Anarcho-Fascism

ANARCHO-FASCISM

NATURE REBORN

BY

JONAS NILSSON

LOGIK FÖRLAG

Originally published as *Anarko-fascism: Naturen återfödd* (2017)
Cover Design: Andreas Nilsson
ISBN: 978-91-88667-19-9

©2017 Logik Förlag
Box 22120, 250 23 Helsingborg, Sweden
www.logik.se | www.logikpub.com
kontakt@logik.se

CONTENTS

Foreword

The idea for this book, and the concept of anarcho-fascism as a label for this line of thought, was born when I wrote my graduation thesis in political science, "Libertarianism meets authoritarianism – The union of fascism and anarchy."[1] The investigative study of the thesis was built on an analysis of ideas, which offered a deeper and more understandable explanation for why so many so-called extremist right-wing fascists and freedom-loving anarcho-capitalists both supported Donald Trump's bid for the presidency. In the thesis, I asserted that this convergence was an expression of what might be labeled "anarcho-fascism." The two political ideological universes were united in their efforts to preserve the worldview and way of life of each. To the political anarchist, freedom must be obtained at the expense of said freedom; The limiting of interaction with non-compatible externals ensures that the in-group can live freely without being devoured by a hostile authoritarian

---

[1] Available in Swedish here: http://www.diva-portal.org "När det frihetliga möter det auktoritära: Föreningen av fascism och anarki" (2016).

7

collective that lacks Western values. To the fascist, on the other hand, freedom must be ensured internally, within the in-group, in order to become a vital and competitive unit against these external forces.

It makes sense when a marketing optimization perspective is applied to the political – providing that the political is recognized as operator-based, the source of the relationship. A relationship that may be harmonious as well as antagonistic.

From this perspective, state formation must be as small and as large as possible at the same time. There is a link here to the Founding Fathers of the United States, who were also the authors of the Constitution. The state apparatus needs to be small enough that the citizens can overthrow it, should it become tyrannical, while also being large enough to be able to defend itself against and guaranteeing freedom from hostile external agents.

Political theories use contemporary times as a jumping-off point, and can only be fully understood in that context. Politics offers something, a solution to an observed problem – politics is the means, the course of action through which the in-groups' interests are met. Thus, political theories build on a contemporary need for reform – Thomas Hobbes using Leviathan as a counterweight to the civil war, to prevent a war of all against all. John Locke promoted the idea of limited government involvement, in order to free the citizens from the rule of arbitrary leadership. Ayn Rand's philosophy emerged as a counter to the utterly unnatural communist ideology.

It is possible that all these people were considered extreme by their contemporaries – because they sought to move society in the opposite direction of its current course. They paved the way, or at least tried to pave the way, for the societal pendulum to swing full force in the other direction, as far away as possible from what they identified as the biggest problems of their time. One might want to consider that the further away from the harmful starting point we get, the more difficult it will become to revive that which needed to die.

This book is also presented as a reaction against a system that cannot possibly, by principal, sustain itself, and thus lacks any *raison d'être*. The political ideas presented in this book must therefore be put into a contemporary societal context to be fully understood, even though the book also implicitly uses anthropology as a starting point.

All political theories move from the abstract to the factual, when the philosophical foundation manages to shape and influence people's lives, a process that in turn affects society as a whole. Political theory/philosophy has always preceded major changes in society, where the existing belief systems have been razed and replaced by new ones.

All human beings live by their belief system, their philosophy, whether they know it or not, and whether they want to or not. This determines how we view ourselves and the world around us, and the belief system is the instrument by which we choose our direction in life. It makes us act or remain passive, to do one thing or another. The belief system differentiates right from wrong, separates good and evil. The way in which social values are shaped and reshaped, and the way governing bodies should be structured, also rests on a philosophical foundation that transcends politics. Anthropology and the human aspect form the basis for the issues of political theories, which, implicitly or explicitly, question whether human beings are fundamentally good or evil, dangerous or harmless.

It is not just about the opposing anthropological viewpoints on whether man is a potentially hazardous creature that must be controlled for his own good, or, if man must be set free in order to flourish. It is more multidimensional than that. Human beings are, in many ways, a uniform species, where everyone can gather around the least common denominator, but mankind is also comprised of a multitude of races and sexes. The right answer for one person may not be right for another. However, this does not mean that every political entity can construct its own reality; it simply stipulates the way in which they need to relate to reality in order not just to survive, but also to be competitive. Only the perception of reality can be constructed, and the dissonance between that which has been constructed and factual reality determines how successful and enduring the culture or civilization will be over time, and in connection with external parties. The survival ratio of the political entity depends on the fusion of biology and culture, adapted to the group's external environment. The optimization is not just in the general compliance, but also depends on the adaptability of the unit when unforeseen changes occur, which will unavoidably happen at some point. To that end, structural flexibility as well as general alertness is required. This book was written primarily for these reasons, because it is disclosure by way of flexibility that can deliver the answers needed to deal with sudden events.

And this is where our current societal problems lie – the older generation, which is the cause of our current situation, is voluntarily blind to the new circumstances that have arisen due to the answers they have delivered. These answers are harmful to us, because they make up a theory that does not harmonize with its actual execution.

The seriousness of the consequences remains to be seen, depending on the magnitude and impact of the false theory.

A faulty realm of thought imposed with blind conviction is inherently evil, because it poses a danger to society and puts us all at risk. One is reminded of the Norse god Odin, and his advice to mortals for virtuous living: *When you come upon misdeeds, speak out against them, and give your enemies no peace.*[2]

The book is divided into three parts: What is false ("The Lie"), what the consequences of this will be ("War"), and how society can be reorganized to make sure this does not happen again ("The State").

Jonas Nilsson
April, 2017

---

[2] See *Hávamál*, verse 127.

THE LIE

Adolf Hitler warned about what he called "the big lie" in *Mein Kampf*:

> All this was inspired by the principle—which is quite true within itself—that in the big lie there is always a certain force of credibility; because the broad masses of a nation are always more easily corrupted in the deeper strata of their emotional nature than consciously or voluntarily; and thus in the primitive simplicity of their minds they more readily fall victims to the big lie than the small lie, since they themselves often tell small lies in little matters but would be ashamed to resort to large-scale falsehoods. It would never come into their heads to fabricate colossal untruths, and they would not believe that others could have the impudence to distort the truth so infamously. Even though the facts which prove this to be so may be brought clearly to their minds, they will still doubt and waver and will continue to think that there may be some other explanation. For the grossly impudent lie always leaves traces behind it, even after it has been nailed down, a fact which is known to all expert liars in this world and to all who conspire together in the art of lying.
>
> — Adolf Hitler,
> *Mein Kampf*, vol. I, ch. X

A lie that is constantly repeated will, in the end, be assimilated by indoctrination into a truth, even by those who humiliate themselves by silent consent, against their own better knowledge. The silence and the repetition corrupt them and make them complicit in maintaining the viability of the lie. To others, those who are dependent on the lie, it is rather pleasant and provides them with a false sense of harmony. The lie becomes part of their self-image and affirms their identity, which can in turn explain their actions. They will defend their identity by any means possible. He who threatens the lie, thereby threatens the ones who believe it. The liars will dismiss you, ostracize you, if you dare to use the truth to shake the illusion the lie has placed them in. The ostracism, the Facebook blocks, give further life to the illusion, because they make it possible for the participants to concur with their own group, and devote themselves to the lie without friction or reality checks. However, this route cannot be sustained; the viability of the lie depends on the ability to shut out the consequences of the lie – but when reality comes knocking, the truth will once more let itself be known. The lie can only be sustained as long as the state is strong enough to absorb its negative consequences and hide them from the citizens.

The Outer Perimeter

The lie provides fictitious answers, and this puts the community at perpetual risk. we are going to have a rude awakening. 200 years of peace have led the Swedes to falsely believe that it is not men in particular that are needed to defend us against a potential attacker. The lack of threats has resulted in the Swedish Armed Forces being ideologically governed, oriented towards extreme feminism, making gender and political correctness more important than actual defense capabilities. If you do not agree with the leftist propaganda, in the shape of the joint "basic values" concerning gender equality and "the equal value of all people", then you will not be welcome in the Armed Forces, regardless of merit. The Armed Forces explicitly strive for a 50/50 gender balance.[1] An ambition that will be realized in the future, through a new (2017) gender-neutral drafting law. The lack of existential threats has as its result that women are now able to play being warriors.

The lie is so deeply ingrained in the citizenry, in particular the naïve, younger female population fervently believes that sexes do not exist, they actually believe that a constructed balance of power between men and women is being upheld by the patriarchy through social reproduction.

Fooling women into thinking that they are as equally capable as men when it comes to defending themselves and performing ultimate acts of violence has to be the most misogynistic political pressure that has ever been exercised. A total reduction of women into being nothing more than really bad copies of men. The most physically accomplished women compete on par with the weakest men in the same category, whether it is boxing, soccer or tennis.

The complete feminization of the Armed Forces has caused a dissonance in the way war is conducted. Carl von Clausewitz stressed that war needs popular passion. If a society lacks men willing to take up arms, that will have a negative affect on the nation's general ability to

---

[1] Försvarsmaktens jämställdhetsplan 2009-2011, HKV beteckning: 16 150:52403, p. 11

wage war. Likewise if the morale and will to fight is not there. The actual fight begins with resistance; otherwise it is just assault and battery. Should a military attack occur under these circumstances, there will be no war, just the occupation of a people completely at the mercy of their attacker.

To fill the war machine's needs and invoke the lust for battle, all one has to do is draw from the male need for self-realization, as the defense of our own kind is an innate need for most men. We are prepared to kill and die for our own political unit, i.e. the tribe, which is based on a common identity. Battles are fought to defend the in-group's interests, and from an evolutionary viewpoint, to secure one's own genetic survival. No man would allow an external threat to attack his family without first having to go through him. This is the very foundation of masculinity, from which all other aspects of masculinity emanate. To deviate from this would be regarded as such cowardice as to render the whole concept of being a man obsolete. He would have utterly forfeited his right to be called a man.

Thus, men also fight in order to be recognized as men, and women have played an important role in that social reproduction. One of the most visible examples of this was the so-called white feather movement in Britain during the First World War. Through social pressure, women tried to compel men to enlist, by handing out white feathers as a sign of cowardice to all men not in uniform. This is a very concrete example of how evolutionary factors drive men to want to fight, on an individual level. Very few women want to be with a man not regarded as such by others, a coward, an outsider, because that would mean that she would also be regarded as beyond the pale – a stigma much harder to handle for women than for men. This leaves men with two options: if they choose not to fight for the women, they will not be able to mate with them, and that leads to a genetic dead end for the man. Or, they can join other men on war expeditions and risk their own lives, but if they survive their genes will live on through the women they mate with upon returning home. This is the biological interplay between the sexes – men like to fight, and women like men who fight for them.

Military historian and theorist Martin van Creveld described this phenomenon as women needing men the most when threatened by other men, and men needing women most when they want to have children.[2]

If this is taken into consideration, the Swedish Armed Forces' recruitment campaign of 2016 is nothing short of delusional. The campaign wants to send a signal to the Swedish political left that the Armed Forces are the "good guys" – tolerant and inclusive. However, the battlefield is not a place where embracing diversity and a "live-and-let-live-mentality" work very well. That is the female survival strategy: to survive as an individual by avoiding vital confrontations. This is how women have survived throughout history. They lie on their backs, voluntarily or involuntary, but they do not fight to the death. That has been reserved for the men. But to imply, as this campaign does, that men are ready to give their lives for others to defend their right to behave any way they like, is nothing if not a feminized and distorted view of male self-sacrifice.

Men are ready to die to defend their own in-group. That is the male survival strategy. If we men cannot

---

[2] Van Creveld, Martin (1991) *The transformation of war*, The Free Press, p. 189.

keep the attacking males at bay, it will spell our literal or genetic death, because our women will fall to the victor. However, for the women in the in-group that the men are defending, it may appear from their perspective as if the men are ready to die for someone else – because that is de facto what they are doing for the women. The recruitment campaign thus becomes an institutionalized form of the women's view of the men. In reality, they are sadly mistaken when it comes to men's willingness to die for someone else – it does not extend beyond those identified as their own in-group, and it certainly does not extend to a group that openly despises everything that can be labeled as masculine.

Even though I am a patriot, or rather, because I am a patriot, considering that one of the patriot's foremost obligations is to protect his people from its own government, I myself am not welcome to join in the defense of my own country. This is due to the fact that I do not share the corrupt set of values that, according to the campaign, is the primary objective of the Armed Forces to defend. The primary objective of the Armed Forces is apparently no longer to defend Sweden, but rather, to act as an advocate for the so-called civil rights of women and other minorities.

Therefore, they can also with ease dismiss any person that might contribute to the country's defense capability, and the Armed Forces have done just that. They did this with the Svea Life Guard soldier Fredrik Hagberg, a spokesperson for the Nordic Youth (Nordisk Ungdom), after he undertook a trip to Ukraine. They did it with Carolus Löfroos, a Finnish Coastal Ranger and Ukraine volunteer, who is no longer welcome as a Home Guardsman. The official security threat to Sweden, and the very reason that we at least formally ought to have a working defense, is the threat from the East, but to have actual combat experience against this enemy is by all accounts not a desirable qualification. The same goes for me, despite my having served in the Swedish military, have experience from the French Foreign Legion and as an assistant instructor in the Azov Battalion in Ukraine, working together with the well-known volunteer Mikael Skillt.

To an outsider it must be confusing to realize that a job interview can end abruptly when the recruiter realizes that the cadet is actually willing to fight for his country, and says: "Sorry. You are not what we are looking for." And then proceed to glance at a poster of two pretty girls posing in uniform, wearing the beret of the Royal Marines – an elite unit that is supposed to spearhead the Swedish Royal Navy. Sweden has the world's first self-proclaimed "feminist government", and with it came the "feminist Armed Forces."

In actuality, Sweden is defenseless, and that has nothing to do with miniscule defense grants. It is entirely due to the lies.

If a war should break out, and we were faced with an opponent of equal or superior strength, we would not be able to replicate the achievements of our famous Caroleans or those of the brave Finns during the Winter War. In such a case, the Swedish state will no longer be able to uphold the consequences of the lie. To claim otherwise would be as absurd as saying that the outcome of the Winter War would have been the same if the men had stayed at home and the women had been sent to the front. Even if the contra factual was true (in a parallel universe where up is down and ugly is beautiful), such an effort would make it impossible for the Finns to assert themselves in the next conflict. The simple reason for this is that the all-important generation of baby-boomers would never have been born, because most of the nation's eggs would have been destroyed during the war – a war fought primarily, from an evolutionary perspective, to defend the eggs.

A hostile attack on Sweden will result in a draft of 18-year-old girls, along with the men, to defend the Swedish set of values, since it is not the Swedish people that should be defended, nor their place on this earth. A sensible approach to our gender-neutral draft would be to make a distinction, as in the Israeli Army, where the women are placed primarily within the logistics section, the tail, and the men join the fighting units, the teeth, thus creating a whole that no enemy should be able to get past. This will not happen in Sweden, however. Unlike Israel, we have reformed our Armed Forces from the standpoint of ideology, not necessity. The lie that gender does not exist has been institutionalized and marketed by the current elites, and has resulted in young women being indoctrinated and brainwashed into believing things that are obviously erroneous. The madness is complete, and the sexes will thereby not be separated, even in an extreme situation such as war, because that would shatter the worldview of the elites, all the things they have fought for and believed in.

There is a linguistic problem within the soldier profession that has enabled the lie to gain a foothold – the word "soldier". It comes from the word "sold", from the Latin solidus, meaning remuneration, and was implemented when soldiers started getting a regular salary for their services. The soldier profession was born, one who carries arms for a living. An army in the field was, whenever possible, accompanied by a logistical tail comprised of women and artisans, constituting a small, mobile community for the army. Towards the end of the 19th century, this "tail" was also incorporated directly under the control of the Armed Forces and its hierarchy, and the services formerly provided by private entrepreneurs became part of the soldier profession. Unfortunately, the reform did not include a linguistic separation between the warrior and the supporter. To be a warrior is more specific than being a soldier. According to the Clausewitzian definition, war is comprised of the very act of violence, and thus, the warrior is someone who projects violence to enforce his will on the enemy, and the person who withstands the enemy's attacks. Therefore, the warrior's domain is that of violence, and all other parts of the Armed Forces exist to provide the warrior with the resources he needs in order to be successful in his acts of violence.

Women as a group are genetically not as well-suited as men when it comes to distributing violence and absorbing violence. They are more easily traumatized than men, physically as well as psychologically. One powerful incident is enough to make a woman develop PTSD (Post Traumatic Stress Disorder). Because women are the indispensable guardians of life, there is an evolutionary explanation for this, namely that women need to react strongly to life-threatening situations in order to stay alive at all cost – it is their very *raison d'être*.

In the event of war, Sweden will not fight, anyway. We have a clear solidarity policy, and when Defense Minister Peter Hultqvist gave a speech to us at the Swedish Defense University in 2015, he was asked why we are taking part in the military effort in Mali. His answer: If we help others, they will help us when we need it. A clear expression of feminized naiveté. We help others where help is not needed, where our efforts will not make any difference one way or another, and in return we expect those we "help" – not to come to our aid, but to fight for us, should we be attacked. We emulate the helpless woman who has to cling to the victorious alpha male, regardless of the outcome. But considering what an annoying little bitch Mother Svea (Sweden) is, we probably should not hold our breath in hopes that someone will actually come to the rescue. What kind of masochist would tolerate us should we be victorious, and what self-respecting nation would allow our post-war historical revisionism, saying that it was actually the Swedish gender-affirmative action policy that led to victory, and had we not had any help we would have won anyway. Most likely Svea's new husband would tell her to shut up and put on a burkha.

This is the reason Trump questioned the United States' role within NATO. The defense alliance ensures co-operation by requiring that two percent of GDP go to the defense budget. A number of NATO members did not meet this requirement, choosing instead to bribe their own citizens with welfare in order to get re-elected, expecting the United States to come to their aid if a threat should arise, thus down-prioritizing the defense budget.

To ensure that co-operation means a joint defense, and not one party being defended by another, Trump should dissolve the two percent-rule and replace it with a demand like that of the Second Amendment to the American Constitution, in relation to the other member states. The right for any and all to bear arms and form militias. That is the only way to determine whether we fight together rather than for each other, or just fight on behalf of one authority in order to wrest control from another. There would then be free men fighting alongside other free men, in the name of liberty.

The heart of the Swedish defense should be free militias, completely detached from central government. That is the only defense system that would not contribute to the classic security dilemma in international relations[3], because it would be a pure defense resource that could not easily be transformed into an offensive force. It also sends a signal that this is not about defending any government authority or set of values – it is a defense for the people, by the people. It would be next to impossible for an external analyst to determine the country's military capability, and that asymmetry would make occupation virtually impossible. Under these conditions, Crimea would never have been occupied without the consent of the Crimeans. Despite this knowledge, Ukraine with its fairly homogenous population of 45 million, appeals to outsiders for help, rather than letting the citizens defend themselves. Instead, citizens are rewarded with 3-7 years in state prison if they choose to defend themselves and others by possessing a Kalashnikov.[4] So, it is either the government asking for help in order to establish its own authority, or, it is the people asking for help because they are not prepared to fight for themselves. Regardless of which, the answer from the West should be the same – we can fight with you, but not for you, and in order to make sure that this is the case, the civil liberties of the citizens must be constitutionally assured. The only thing that should determine defense capability is people's desire to defend themselves. If a person is expected to fight on someone else's behalf, there must be some kind of trade-off. This applies to individuals as well – if women want

---

[3] Escalation to an arms race when both sides mobilize to secure it's defense against the other side's increasing capability.

[4] Article 263 of the Ukrainian Criminal Codex.

men to come to their aid against other malevolent men, they need to start respecting and honoring the masculine traits. The irony here is that while women are incapable of defending themselves, they still believe that they are fit to defend the nation's existence. The female conclusion here is obviously not to start appreciating their men again, but rather, to argue that they have a right not to be attacked in the first place. A right that does not exist if there is no one who is capable, and willing, to uphold it. Women handle conflict by slandering, bullying and ostracism – methods that are already common practice within our "feminist government."

A good friend of mine works at a South American embassy in Stockholm. In a private conversation with the Russian ambassador to Stockholm, my friend asked the ambassador what he thought about the new security situation (this was in 2016). He replied that the biggest change under the Löfven administration (the world's first "feminist government") was that all dialogue had ceased, we no longer talk to each other, and this poses a threat in and of itself, because that increases the risk of misunderstandings and unnecessary escalations. This is new to us, said the ambassador, we have always maintained a dialogue with you, even in the tensest years during the Cold War.

The feminization of our policies and our Armed Forces make up the biggest security threat to Sweden not just in modern times, but through the ages. The verbal bullying and ostracism only work when they are directed at the in-group, those who can be categorized as "we". That is to say – the people who care if they upset you. Outside the "we"-group, that mode of conflict management is not only utterly powerless, but also extremely detached from reality. Arminius could not have cared less about how the conquered peoples felt, when he by use of force made the Rhein the Roman Empire's last outpost in the north.

A people bearing arms, and the abolition of the state's monopoly on violence, would greatly reduce the government's ability to perpetuate the madness that is currently running rampant in Rosenbad (the Swedish Government's offices). The insecurity that women and feminized men would feel towards a population carrying arms would actually make them safer. The illusion that rights exist and danger can be legislated away would evaporate, and then it would be up to them to get real and adapt to actual rather than imagined or desired conditions. Either by getting tough, or by treating the male population with respect and hope that they do not hold a grudge, but are still willing to uphold the security in society. Because this ultimately depends on the good will of the men.

Using Lies as a Weapon

It has also been customary for the ruling elites, hidden within what may be perceived as the majority's rule of terror, to depend on the lie of "everyone's equal worth" in order to shut out individuals, groups, parties and clubs, and deny them financial support – with reference to this abstract, nonsensical concept.

The crazy part about their own contradiction is that they themselves fail to live up to their own epithet, by shutting out anyone pointing to the unreasonableness and falseness of what is being said. The liberal ideals are to be upheld at any cost – even if that means a betrayal of these same liberal ideals. They say that everyone has equal worth, but it is obvious that this only applies to those who subscribe to this lie. Everyone else is shut out, because they in turn wish to shut others out. Democracy only applies to those who want democracy, and so on. Madness. It might be called hypocrisy, but that is not what it is. It is war. Their idea versus our idea. An absolute enmity. Two forces so completely incompatible that only one can survive. If they win, we die by the total annihilation of the "us". The fight is existential.

Politics is antagonistic. It is always waged one against another. Their perception of politics as "together" is an exclusion and elimination of "us". Policies are not decided by us, they are used against us, and they cannot be used against "them" because that would annihilate their view of politics as a joint expression that we implement together.

This is why we are shut out. It has nothing to do with "all men being equal." They know that when we win, and we will win, they will cease to exist. They will be given no leeway. They will not be able to live like parasites of the body of society anymore. They will, gasp, be forced to support themselves by offering something that has an actual worth. Some will not even have to worry about that because, hopefully, they will be deported.

This is what separates us from them. We do not disguise ourselves and our goals. We do not hide behind impossible tenets and pretend to be good. We are good, and that is precisely why we point out evil things. This is the reason they fear us. We cannot be bought or blackmailed into submission. They know this, and because neither rope nor swords work as a threat, only exclusion is left as a weapon.

The historian Robert Conquest pointed to a "law of politics": if a political movement is not explicitly right wing extremist, or what our enemies term "neo-Nazi", that movement will in time turn to the left and become more socialist than it originally was. These are the bribable, those who can be let in, because they do not pose a threat. Not even if they came to power, because by then they will have turned to the dark side. This will happen through their own corruption; their repetition of the enemy's lies has made them blind to what is actually true or false, good or evil.

Thus, it is a blessing in disguise to anyone affected by the left wing liberal tyranny. There can be no doubt who the enemy is in a situation like that. The political enemy must be clear, and you sign your own death warrant if you make yourself dependent on your enemy. For this reason, I was not terribly upset when the Sweden Democrats' youth organization SDU was denied financial support, or when Kent Ekeroth (now an SD-parliamentarian) was booted from his internship at the Swedish embassy in Israel in 2006. These things make the politics real, they strip away any blinders and illusions about what is going on. As a reminder of this, I have posted my rejection slip from the National Home Guard on my refrigerator door – a rejection motivated by my not passing the "security clearance." This makes me an admitted enemy; our enmity is out in the open.

If, on the other hand, support is given, the operator will have entered into a symbiosis with the enemy. The operator's struggle to maintain support will at the same time implicitly become a struggle to preserve our enemy. In a best-case scenario, this will bring about new leadership, but change in and of itself is not our goal. We do not simply want to burn down the house, it has to burn, and we cannot be inside when that happens. To do something like that you would have to be an absolute madman, someone who wants to see everything burn and is prepared to burn with it. This phenomenon has thus far only been observed within the European Union, a project that exists in the twilight zone between inter-state and supranational federation. However, the opposition within the European Union, with the pan-European party APF (Alliance for Peace and Freedom) working to dissolve the union entirely, has not seen its equivalent on a nation-state level. To then view it as a victory when some "oppositional" political "force" gains life support from press subsidies or some other lethal injection to its own activities, not even forced on them by their enemies but rather, bizarrely, actively coveted by some so-called oppositionals, is nothing short of self-delusion. This is not an awakening; it is a funeral.

The goal of these entities is then no longer what they themselves claim – final victory. Instead, the entire *raison d'être* becomes to meet the demands and criteria in order to gain the financial support. This becomes the actual goal, disguised as means to an end – which would require the slaughter of their own golden calf. And that will never happen. They are lured into the trap like the prey of the poisonous Mexican snake Cantil. This snake has a tail that looks just like a tasty little worm, fooling the prey into thinking they are in for a nice snack, when in fact all they will get a taste of is the snake's venom. The same applies on an individual level: people on social welfare are reduced to nothing more than breeding machines and election cattle for the left. Bought and paid for.

Therefore, it is very pleasing to see that a self-supporting and market-friendly opposition is gaining momentum. Unlike an opposition dependent on various forms of aid and benefits, it draws power from its consumers and not from our enemy. Not having to adapt to the enemy's rules to get aid optimizes operations towards the end goal. In the case of media opposition, that goal is to convey a message to as many people as possible. Two good examples of this are the podcast Motgift and the publishing house Logik, which published the book you are now reading, among others. Their goal is different from, say, the newspaper Nya Tider, whose primary goal is to meet the criteria for press subsidies in order to stay alive. This dependency affects efficiency. Without the drug, the fix, they will perish. The paper has six full-time employees, plus a few part-timers and freelance writers. The total work required to produce this weekly paper and deliver it to its 4000 subscribers is about 300 hours. That means about 20 minutes of work for each person reached per week. Compare that to the podcast Motgift, which is a two-hour show, plus about ten hours of preparations – and they have tens of thousands of listeners. Therein lies the difference between adapting to the market or conforming to the rules in order to get subsidies. And, for those of you who find the comparison unfair because the forums are different, talk radio versus newspaper, a comparison to the alternative web magazines Fria Tider and Nyheter Idag would be even more devastating. They reach hundreds of thousands of readers every week, with substantially less staff and overhead costs than the subsidized Nya Tider.

In fact, the press subsidy is corruption of power at its finest, because it links the media to political power, thus ensuring a stranglehold around the public's neck. No paper will ever bite the hand that feeds it, and no party can seriously question the press subsidy without being discredited in the media, thereby losing the all-important media influence that is usually required to seize power.

Our exclusion from the mainstream media as well

as the political establishment has forced us to build parallel structures – and it is through our alternative channels that we have a chance to tear down the old and start something new, without being buried in the rubble ourselves.

The fake oppositionals, however, surrender and adhere to the rules set by the enemy. To make matters worse, these rules are not static, but can be bent when needed, in order to fight you in particular. To know your enemy fully, you must understand the concept of absolute enmity. Your undoing is the only principle that matters in the end, everything else is just white noise that justifies their working towards your destruction – like the claims that you do not respect that "all men are equal" or "democratic values." This is nonsense. They want your death, and to fight you they must portray you as evil. If you support yourself financially and do not accept any lethal "life support", if you accept the fact that you are one of "the others" and these people are not part of your tribe, that they are your enemies – then these epithets will hold no power over you.

Political "Togetherness"

Those who can make you believe absurdities,
can make you commit atrocities – Voltaire

Politics is waged one against another. It is the interaction and the conflict that arise when different interests collide, and the further away from each other these interests lie, the more absolute and filled with conflict politics will be. Therefore there is a crucial difference between the private enemy and the political enemy.

The private enemy falls into the category of personal quarrel, within the in-group; it is an argument that the Christian faith teaches us to resolve by turning the other cheek and taking the high road. This can be done, since the private enemy does not affect your life more than you let him, and holds no political sway over you. The private enemy cannot dictate your life through legislation and appropriation directions.

Carl Schmitt defined political interaction as friend/enemy relationship. The distinction is a criterion and not a definition of content. It should be understood as a number of independent antitheses that cannot be further derived, like the moral concepts of good and evil and the aesthetic concepts of beautiful and ugly.[5]

Politics cannot be understood if the individual unit does not understand who will suffer the consequences and who needs to be fought. So the political does not only have a semantic connection to the polemical; it is also factual. The political enemy does not have to be evil or ugly, but is quite simply "the other", someone with whom it may in fact be economically beneficial to interact. But "the other", "the enemy", or perhaps more poignantly, "the stranger", whose nature negates your way of living, can cause an existential conflict, and become an enemy that must be fought to preserve your way of life.

Unlike the private enemy, the quarrel, the political enemy can be dealt with successfully without emotion – the political attack is wholly impersonal, it is strictly business when the killing blow is dealt to an opponent. The political enemy is made up of a group

---

[5] Schmitt, Carl (2007), *The Concept of the Political*, Chicago: University of Chicago Press.

that is in conflict with your own political entity. One group fighting another group, which means the friend/ enemy distinction must be understood literally, not metaphorically. The magnitude of the gap between the political goals of the respective groups, and their desire to achieve them, determine the intensity of the conflict. This in turn determines whether the interaction with "the other" is antagonistic or harmonious. When the interests of the two political entities collide and cannot be reconciled, the ultimate consequence will be war, or revolution.

The conflict-filled struggle that is politics should not be perceived as a game of sports, like wrestling, but rather a martial struggle. The insight into politics rests within the frame of understanding that violence is part of the struggle, that there is an actual possibility that people will die somewhere along the line. From that point of view, every political decision rests on the bullet from a rifle waiting to be fired, should the enemy refuse to yield. War and annihilation are the most extreme consequences of such enmity. Political action must be taken against the right party, at the right opportunity and in the right way – too much violence can be just as harmful as a lack thereof. Too much can force the opponent to defend himself physically, and too little can give him precious room to maneuver and thereby harm you.

Israel and the Jewish people have a high degree of understanding concerning not just the political part, but also, that it is one's own tribe that makes up the political unit. They have been highly successful, despite the lack of their own state or geographical space for the greater part of history. The Jews have protected the interests of the in-group, and thereby also taken part in the political process whenever their interests have collided with that of their host population, regardless of where they have found themselves at the time. This has cost them dearly, but it has also ensured their survival, their continued existence. If, on the other hand, they had chosen not to engage in the political struggle, they would have perished – they would have been devoured and integrated into "the other" political unit. Instead of being integrated with "the other", they have fought them, because their furtherance of their own interests has been at the expense of their political opponent in the zero-sum game of power, where irreconcilables collide. Politics is about furthering the interests of your own in-group. In an Aristotelian sense, this is its purpose. And what Schmitt categorized as the "friend-group" is, at its most fundamental level, based on blood. It is the identity that binds a political unit together, and when various artificial identities, based on nurture rather than nature, falter, the default setting is to fall back on the identity that is unchanging – the identity given by nature.

A prime example of this is Rickard Flinga's experiences of prison life in the United States.[6] There, it became clear to him that who you were before you set foot in the place that would dominate the rest of your life did not matter. The group dynamics in prison are not dictated by your interests or political ideology; Liberals do not hang out in one corner and Social Democrats in another. Instead, what separates the different groups is racial background – in order to ensure your own well-being and even survival in an extremely vulnerable situation.

The purpose of politics is to make things better for "us." It is supposed to benefit you as an individual, your

---

[6] Flinga, Rickard. (2005). *Iskallt och stenhårt: mina 20 år i Texas fängelser*, Stockholm: Norstedt.

political unit and your own community, i.e. your own interests. No serious political theorist has ever claimed that your policies should be based on the interests of another group, at the expense of your own. To allow the existence of "the other" to trump your own interests is truly suicidal and will lead to your destruction. A political altruism that feeds on your own suffering is nothing short of madness.

A left-leaning liberal feminist could very well make the argument that if "the others" achieve a better life, that will benefit us down the road as well. This is utterly untrue. If they do not have anything of value to offer us, then they mean nothing to us – they are non-existent. They need us; we do not need them, and if we should start to need them, that means they have something of value to offer us. Then a political negotiation can begin, wherein either something of value is traded for something else, or the hierarchical tyrant/slave-relationship is established to obtain that which is valuable through other means than voluntary surrender.

There is nothing that would make integration worth it to "us." That is to say, they cannot offer us anything of value or threaten us with something we cannot resist. They are nothing. And a mixing of "us" and "them" will lead to our also becoming nothing. If one does not separate the groups in according to the political distinction, it becomes impossible to represent and satisfy the interests of the in-group.

By denying that politics is by nature exclusionary, our own group will cease to exist in favor of another. The left-wing liberal establishment peddle inclusive "politics" that strive to eliminate the polemics of politics by categorizing the policies as activities conducted "together", thus refusing to identify with the in-group because that would make the political friend/enemy relationship a reality.

This is significant to our political struggle and our opponent's struggle to exterminate the "us." A hostile strategic plan against us that knows no boundaries – and it became very clear during the 2016 presidential election campaign in the United States that this is by no means an exclusively Swedish, German, French or British problem. The entire West is under attack – which was made abundantly clear through the Clinton propaganda tagline purporting that we are "Stronger Together."

To fall back in line with this political absurdity opens the door for misdeeds against the in-group that Swedish politicians ought to represent – the Swedes. This is key to understanding the political climate in Sweden today. There is a strong taboo against making the necessary distinction between "us" and "them", because that would go against our self-annihilating lie of "everyone's equal worth."

This absurdity has led to a very visible betrayal of the "us" group – the unwillingness of our judicial system to immediately deport foreign criminals. Prosecutor Daniel Jonsson summed up this attitude very well when he said, quite correctly, that a convicted rapist might just as well revert to crime in his own home country as in Sweden.[7] Thus, no distinction is made between prospective rape victims among Swedish women in Sweden, and say, Somali women in Somalia.

The purpose of the law is that it makes society safer. It is supposed to shield the citizens from external danger

---

[7] Ed. (2013). Våldtog döende kvinna får stanna i Sverige. *Fria Tider*, [online]. Available at:
http://www.friatider.se/valdtog-doende-kvinna-far- stanna-i-sverige
[Accessed 22 Aug. 2017]

through the outer perimeter, the nation's borders, as well as internal dangers such as abuse and fraud. Swedish law does not exist to make sure that African women are not raped by African men. Its jurisdiction does not include Africa. That is not where we should uphold our laws.

The overall consequence of "together" politics, where everyone has the same worth, is that "we" are forced to take responsibility for "them." We are obliged to help them as if they belonged with us. They, on the other hand, know that they do not belong with us and that we (the political opposition) do not belong with them. So, the political lines of conflict are threefold, and the backlash against the political absurdities will eventually rise like a tide and be just as impossible to ignore. The state lacks the strength to absorb this, the most preposterous of lies. The consequences are knocking at the door – ready to disturb the peace.

THE WAR

Do you fear a duel with a Swedish-hating mob?
- Magnus Söderman

Men have a better understanding of the realities of violence than women, due to the fact that they are the foremost practitioners of violence, and so most often are the ones who suffer the most serious and permanent consequence – death. They know the political effect of a decision, that it is a polemic – that it is rife with conflict, and that the purest form of rampant conflict can be found within Clausewitz' ideal war. In the ideal war, the escalation of violence on both sides is only inhibited by the amount of resources available, whatever that may be: The number of troops that can be deployed, the number of cannons that can be manufactured, or how many rounds that can be fired. The closest we have ever gotten to Clausewitz' ideal war is the fully mechanized mass slaughter in the trenches of the First World War. We are not going to analyze what made this fatal escalation possible, but rather, have a look at what prevents unnecessary political escalation, nationally and internationally.

What makes war and conflict rational is the will, interests and goals of the political entity. This is the limiting force of absolute war. These are the factors that decide how much the political entity wants to achieve its goals versus how much it is willing to sacrifice to enforce its will on an enemy. Only this prevents the ideal war from occurring. What makes the calculation fluid is that exactly the same considerations are taken by the opponent – regardless of whether that opponent is inside the country or outside. This means that if the leading political entity in the country puts an enormous amount of resources into caring for "the other", then revolution becomes an inevitability, because in the long run that entails a lower cost for the political party under attack than the degradation and suicide of submission would. Always assuming that the policies are being put forth to benefit the in-group, and that war is the organizing and distributing factor of male aggression – a civilizing measure, if you will. War is also an extension of politics. In that regard, General Ludendorff was right when he pointed out that politics is incidental to war, as both are practiced for the good of the people, but war is the ultimate struggle to survive. If a people is not ready to fight to stay alive and flourish, then it will not do so, except by someone else's good graces. War is the ultimate sign of life, the last measure to stay alive and not perish. To not be prepared to fight is tantamount to being prepared to die without resistance, a prey incapable and unworthy of sustaining life.

If a political entity is pushed hard enough and long enough, that will result in war. If the other political unit is made up of men, that is. Women, on the other hand, can be subjugated and relegated to becoming third-class citizens, without reacting violently in response.

Women may have other means at their disposal; however, violence is not one of them. Saudi Arabia is a prime example of this. Women lack political influence, they are not allowed to drive cars, a woman subjected to rape can be sentenced to death for adultery, and to make matters even worse – they are forced to wear black drapes that cover them from head to toe, to avoid seducing every man they meet. Why do the women accept this? Where is the armed revolution? But above all else; why do Western feminists not act against this perfect incarnation of patriarchy, instead of insisting that the problem is Western men?

The answer lies within the political friend/enemy distinction. The "friend" group of Western women, particularly the feminists, does not include their oppressed sisters in the Middle East, because they only have power over their own group. They are utterly powerless against an external group, with whom there is a concrete risk of conflict. Alas, contemporary feminists can be seen wearing the Islamic veil and heard saying that this is somehow edifying to women, as is apparently shouting 'Allahu Akbar' at their rallies. The reason is, quite simply, that they cannot go after people who do not belong to their own group, at the risk of provoking conflict and also, risking their own peace of mind, which rests on the "together" consensus politics that avoids polemics of every kind. We will see that some Western feminists will even go as far as converting to Islam, claiming that this is an act of empowerment. Some of these women become radicalized and join the Islamic holy war against the West – Jihad.

On the other hand, male slaves have rebelled since the dawn of time, with varying degrees of success. This is because it is in their nature to fight when they are attacked or oppressed. Women, not men, can be pushed very far without starting a revolution. That is why the Arabs castrated their African slaves and remade them into non-men, eunuchs. Through this practice, constant complications and friction in society could be avoided, and control maintained without having to deal with recurring slave insurrections.

The reason Western women have their freedom is because Western men have thought it was a good idea to uphold it. Every authority rests on the capacity for violence in the end. When it comes to resisting authority, as well as trying to exercise it on an unwilling subject.

Everything that is given to you lacks value. If you have not acquired it and are capable of defending it, then it is not yours, other than in the sense that the one who can take it from you lets you have it.

I live in the feminist Mecca of Stockholm. When it became clear that more men backed Donald Trump over Hillary Clinton, a "male" postgraduate student at my alma mater, the Swedish Defense University, questioned whether men should really be allowed to vote, or if we would be better off with just women voting. Pathetic. If it had been the other way around, and someone said that women should not be allowed to vote because they tend to vote to the left and for big government, it would have been the end of that person's academic career.

The reason why women get upset when there is talk of stripping them of their voting rights is that this right was given to them, and was not conquered by them. If they are not allowed into political life, then they as a collective will have no say in what happens politically. Instead, their political influence will be individual and unofficial, via networking and scheming. For example, a king's or courtier's mistress can act as a lobbyist for other interests.

Men, on the other hand, are not nearly as insulted if someone questions men's right to vote; a man would not even take the sentiment seriously – especially if it came from a woman or feminized man. Why? Because a woman cannot strip him of his right to vote, and a feminized man who cannot even stand up to women could not possibly stand up to a man that can. A man can also, whenever he chooses, shift his political influence from the voting ballot to the barrel of a gun. Voting is a kind of political pressure, i.e. violence. When a political entity stops exercising political influence via voting, and instead chooses to exert influence by other means, it will not matter anymore who has the most votes. The political winners will depend on things other than counting the votes.

This is the reason men have universal suffrage – the male potential for violence. To avoid a revolution, the Swedish king struck a deal regarding the absolute power he had previously held, and chose to share it with other political entities who might otherwise have forced him out of power altogether. What followed was a kind of semi-war, when the power of authority shifted from the aristocracy to the male population in general. The Swedish constitution of 1809 replaced the royal autocracy in accordance with the principle of separation of powers that had become dominant in the West.[1] The understanding of the lines of political conflict meant that Sweden was democratized without armed struggle – unlike, for instance, France and the United States. One might

---

[1] Today, Sweden has no division of powers, and we are totally at the mercy of the people via the Parliament. According to the 1974 Instrument of Government, which replaced the one from 1809, popular sovereignty rules, and the first paragraph of the Instrument of Government reads; "All public power in Sweden proceeds from the people."

say that the death of the king of France allowed the Swedish king to live. We, the Swedish people and the Swedish king, managed to compromise, because both parties believed that this was preferable to risking a costly war with an uncertain outcome.

The feminized society lacks insight into the violent polemics between different groups. Therefore, feminized policies will be implemented without considering the possibility of a violent backlash. Instead, they will act as if other groups do not exist, and engage in conflict management designed for their own unit – and ostracize any and all parties that do not agree with them. There is no understanding of the fact that any political decision may ultimately lead to either war or revolution. That scenario does not exist in their universe, as they lack any insight into how violence and politics work. When everything revolves around women, it all becomes about subjecting your antagonists to ostracism, emotional blackmail or psychological bullying, none of which leads to a violent backlash. Such policies will inevitably lead to war sooner or later, provided that there are men involved.

The foundation of democracy is the common identity that the people and their leaders share. If the people and its leaders act as *one*, the law practically writes itself. Rousseau paints a picture of this in *Contrat Social*. However, this identity does not have to be established via voting rights, which have nevertheless become synonymous with democracy – as if democracy, the rule of the people, would be impossible without voting rights. In this regard, fascism is closer to the democratic condition than today's modern Western democracy, because fascism is based on a common identity. This is not the case when it comes to the elected Swedish government. The dissonance between the "Swedish" political leaders and the Swedish people has never been greater. The leaders even deny the very existence of a Swedish identity. But what the feminized Swedish establishment should really be worried about is not the opposition they are ostracizing, but what comes after that. Everyone who still has the ability to hear – hear us roar, and take heed – we exist! And this is not a question that is up for debate; it is a question that will be acted out. The pendulum will swing back like a sledgehammer, a sledgehammer that will crush everything in its way.

"Swedish" political leaders have attempted to dissolve the political unit they should be representing – the Swedes – through a humiliating migration policy where we, the Swedes, are stripped of the *right* to our own country. As I have pointed out before, however, rights do not exist, and anything that is bestowed lacks value. Hermann Göring formulated this eternal truth in Germany Reborn: "Destiny never forgives the man who without struggle abandons that which a generous providence has placed in his hands. 'What you have inherited from your forefathers you must win anew in order to keep it.'"[2]

If the question is to whom does the country belong, then the answer is very simple: it belongs to the political entity that is prepared and able to fight for the country, to conquer it, and has the necessary potential for violence to keep it.

It is through the ability and willingness to defend what you have that you make sure it is yours. This goes without saying, and is echoed in Thomas Jefferson's famous statement "The tree of liberty must be refreshed from

---

[2] Göring, H. (1934). *Germany Reborn*. London: E. Mathews & Marrot.

time to time with the blood of patriots and tyrants."

If you are not prepared to fight and bleed for what you have, and to spill the blood of those who seek to take it from you, then you have nothing. You are a dead man walking. Everything he has and holds dear lacks value, because he is not prepared to kill or be killed to defend his loved ones. Such a man exists purely by the grace of another, someone who is *in fact* ready to make these sacrifices.

The feminized Swedish establishment avoids identifying an enemy, because that would point to a political reality behind the polemics. That would inevitably bring about a confrontation. And they avoid this because of our violent past – they are afraid of who we are. They fear the lengths that a man will go to in order to defend himself and his loved ones against an attacker. They want a safe and comfortable life more than anything. However, we have never been as unsafe as we are now. We have never been as close to extinction as we are now. To quote Christoffer Ragne (VAM – Vitt Ariskt Motstånd, White Aryan Resistance): "Our nation is committing racial suicide."[3]

There is a notion that violence is always wrong, in every situation. This is one of the great taboos of our time, and it will bear rotten fruit when violence becomes necessary for us to defend ourselves. Compare the modern-day feminized Swedish man to what he once was: a free man who was required to fight when necessary, with the understanding that death on the battlefield was the only road that lead to Valhalla. The most important quality a warrior can have is not that

---

[3] Words spoken by Ragne in his defense, during a trial regarding a bank robbery in order to finance the struggle. The words became legendary, and immortalized on the music album *Death to ZOG*, where the phrase was used as an introduction to the song *Death to ZOG*.

he is prepared to kill – but that he himself is prepared to die and has made his peace with death. According to Frederick the Great, this is what makes men march side by side to the thundering sound of cannon fire. A fallen comrade of mine, my leader, Eugène Terre'Blanche (AWB, Afrikaner Resistance Movement) said to me: "If it comes to war, we will all die. But, what better death could a man have than when facing fearful odds, for the ashes of his fathers, and the temples of his Gods?"[4]

Glory and honor are concepts that must be restored. Men have always been imbued with these concepts, which have manifested themselves through action. It is like the Spartan woman told her man before he went off to war – come home with your shield, or on it. The shield was a guarantor that the man had not broken the Hoplite phalanx and run from the battlefield. The ultimate outcome of such a shameful deed, to throw away your shield and run, would be that Sparta would be left defenseless. Sparta lacked protective walls; their defense was the men, and the wall that all Spartans depended on was their shields. Sweden, on the other hand, lacks walls as well as men.

The feminized man is an honorless product of our time, created by the most cowardly generation of Swedes ever to walk this earth. If nothing is done, they will go down in history as the last Swedes, spineless creatures whose only defense against evil men was to claim their right not to be attacked. "Violence is wrong, stop hitting us, stop raping us!" But why do you not defend yourselves?

---

[4] I remember this like it was yesterday, when Terre'Blanche uttered these words to me one late afternoon on his farm close to Ventersdorp, the same farm where he was brutally murdered two years later. He lived and died by this quote. Rest in peace. Originally, the quote was taken from the poem *Horatius*.

"That is not the problem, the problem is that someone is attacking us, the problem is patriarchy!" They say this without realizing that they are attacking the only thing that could protect them – a masculine elite. That is the only reason we have evolved and still exist as a species.

If you want to see a feminist become offended, all you have to do is point out this fact to her. If you are not willing or capable of defending yourself, someone else will have to do it. Remember: women need men at the most when they are threatened by other men; hence the command of the Spartan women, urging their men to return with their shields. But a modern-day feminist will not reason along these lines; she believes that she has a "right" not to be attacked by men. She calls for a better defense against men, while in a shrill voice shrieking for more equality with – men. That paradoxical antithesis will ensure that we make absolutely no progress in any direction, because the two circumstances rule each other out.

The parliamentary branch of the Sweden-friendly movement, the Sweden Democrats (SD), has chosen to fight the replacement of the Swedish people through their migration policy program, which advocates a politicized "Open Swedishness." The thought behind this is that anyone can become Swedish, if he or she chooses to live as a Swede, whatever that means. This is an Americanized view of migration, with the idea of the West and its values at its core. But in this respect, being Swedish goes deeper than being an American. I was born a Swede and I will die a Swede, regardless of how I choose to live my life. Thus, "Open Swedishness" is a totally unreasonable concept. Of what does this Swedishness consist – the consensus culture? The Law of Jante? This is a Swedishness that I will fight until the day I die, and that will not make me any less of a Swede. Sure, this might be a *ruse de guerre* of unprecedented proportions, a war strategy worthy that of Odin, to pretend that the foreign hordes will be assimilated into the present day wussy Swedish culture, which has no room for men, thus allowing SD to disarm and mentally pacify an antagonist that must, in the end, be driven out. In my view it is highly unlikely that such a hidden agenda exists, though.

That is why the rebirth of American nationalism with Trump's ascension to power was invaluable to Europe as well as America. The transmission and positive reciprocation of nationalism between the continents is easiest when it flows from America to Europe, not the other way around. This is due to the fact that nationalism in Europe is impossible to distinguish from the nation, i.e. its ethnic population. The Sweden Democrats have chosen to Americanize the view of migration in this regard, and talk about Swedes as if they were an idea that other people can adapt to and thus become Swedish themselves.

War knows no boundaries and is also more often than not impossible to separate from migration. The difference between war and migration is, according to the former Governor of Louisiana, Bobby Jindal (2008-2016), that the immigrants assimilate.[5] Therefore, immigration without intention of assimilation is an act of war. This is consistent with the idea that the United States was founded on, as well as the Open Swedishness promoted by the Sweden Democrats.

---

[5] Mchugh, Katie. (2015). *Breitbart* [online], "Bobby Jindal: 'Immigration whitout assimilation is an invasion'", Available at: http://www.breitbart.com/ big-government/2015/11/04/bobby-jindal-immigration-without- assimilation-is-an-invasion/ [Accessed 22 Aug. 2017]

Large immigrant groups in Sweden as well as the rest of Europe do not strive to assimilate, and why should they? They want to preserve their way of life, and movement across geographic borders does not change the instinct of self-preservation connected with one's own political unit. On the contrary, our leftist/liberal idea of multiculture is in direct opposition to the idea of assimilation. Because the liberal political ideal is "togetherness," there can be no "us" to assimilate into. Instead, "the other" political unit is institutionalized through subsidies. We are creating a political animosity through our desire for "together"-politics. The leftist liberal hegemony lacks an understanding of its own political unit, and will therefore lose against those who carry out the actual political struggle.

An ice hockey team that does not discriminate between their own team and the opposing team is bound to lose. If you want success, you can only play together with members of your own team, i.e. the "friend" group as defined by Schmitt within the friend/enemy dichotomy.

The effect of large population displacements is the same as in war – a new political entity takes over where another has previously been in control of the geographical space. A new way of life takes over, a new rule, but above all there is a new people. The physical country may still be there, but it no longer exists as it once did, and it never will again if the indigenous population disappears for good. This is the ultimate consequence of trying to merge two peoples whose respective political philosophies make them incompatible. It is the foundation of absolute enmity, where there can only be one winner and no compromise is possible. There is only fight, win and live, or, avoid the necessary confrontation and die, not just for now, but forever.

In other words – migration is war, because it will lead to our extinction or the obliteration of our way of life. Or both.

The foremost example of this up until now, is our own Great Migration Period. Not only did we stop the Romans in the Teutoburg Forest in 9 CE, we proceeded to crush the Roman Empire, not just through armed force, but also through migration. It was a displacement of nations that crushed everything that had gone before and replaced it with another way of life, despite the fact that the Germanic tribes were considered barbarians by the more civilized and technologically superior Romans.

An invasion does not only take place through the advance of armed soldiers. Throughout history it has happened either in connection with or after settlements have been established by the new population. Sometimes this has been the actual purpose of the war – to procure the land. The creation of new living space at the expense of another through violence. However, as the case is now, no one objects to another people expanding their living space, so no violence is necessary – it is a walkover. The migration wave today does not need soldiers to pave the way for them, because our leftist liberal establishment has denied us and included them. The migration is not even a war strategy like a Trojan Horse; it is treachery, pure and simple. The shepherd has opened the gate to the wolves, under the pretence that all animals *should* get along. And in this case, this will also affect the shepherd himself, because no wolf will distinguish between sheep and shepherd, and no wolf recognizes the authority of the shepherd.

Historically, it has been less relevant to the women which side wins the war, skirmish or raid. A conquest has *only* meant an adjustment to new masters. And all through human evolution, up until recently, it most often meant a new man from a neighboring tribe, which means inter-tribal exchange where blood, language and culture have been similar. There is most likely a biological conditioning when it comes to women's lower degree of loyalty to the in-group. Psychological research shows that women tend to counter threats with a "tend-and-befriend" strategy, to ensure their own survival.[6] This makes it hard for women to understand politics, and the constant risk of war, because they are the winners' trophies, not the victims. However, the conflict that is ongoing now will lead to a change for the worse, providing that we men do not end the feminized madness that is threatening to dissolve our own group.

Muslims are fanatical opponents of assimilation into the Western way of life. They create no-go zones, implement sharia law as far as possible, and are governed by their mosque rather than the law of the land. A mosque that by the way more often than not is financed by Saudi Arabia. A country that is geographically, culturally and racially close to the migrants, but does not accept a single migrant from the massive hordes that are on the move. The refugees are like pawns on a chessboard to the Saudis. The refugees themselves could very well be unaware of their geopolitical role, because they might just be fleeing to a more economically lucrative West, where the welfare flows like the nectar of the Olympian gods. In addition to being parasites, they also make up the determining factor of Islam's expansion ambitions, financed and forced upon us by the Saudis, among others.

---

[6] Taylor, et al (2000). "Biobehavioral responses to stress in females: tend-and-befriend not fight-or-flight". *Psychological Review.* Vol 107, No 3, p. 411 – 429.

Because authority can be derived from the potential for violence, the migrants do not need to achieve very large numbers before they begin to exert political pressure. In this case, the political pressure is segregation, and establishing their own authority over that of the state. We can already see that they have achieved this in the so-called exclusion areas, where the long arm of the law has become short and impotent. Swedish law is on its knees, pleading for respect for what we ourselves have subsidized and financed, hoping that they will see reason and respect us so we can all live together.

We are in the midst of a power struggle, a battle that our nation is refusing to fight – we will not fight, and will therefore be killed. Social welfare has become our nation's tribute, bestowed upon those who occupy us in the hopes that it will create a "we" together with people who wish our political or actual death.

The migration crisis will lead to the war of our generation. Not a war in a conventional sense, but one that will differ significantly from the Clausewitzian trinity consisting of the people, the military and politics, between two or more parties depending on the constitution. All these elements will merge and dissolve, not just from one side, but from all sides. The leftist liberal side, which makes up the establishment, will be stuck in the Clausewitzian model and unable to handle the threat they are faced with – which will mean certain death. It will be a return to the way that war was fought before it became synonymous with government activities. Decentralized, tribal and anarchistic, but also in this case, without a counterpart to make peace with – absolute enmity cannot possibly contain any room for compromise. War can, however, be fought with the ambition of staging a *coup d'état* in an attempt to gain control of the state, but the war itself will not be for the benefit of the state and its main components will not be part of it. Above all, the fundamental pillars, the very *raison d'être* of the state, will be fought to the point that the state as we know it will cease to exist.

Therefore, war is a better word than "political struggle" to describe what is to come. Politics is one party against another, and that is not our ambition. We have chosen to defend ourselves against this. War is simply an act, a means to an end, and when there is no possibility of compromise, given that our existence is not negotiable, the only feasible outcome is escalation until one side backs down. To the liberal left-wing establishment, this means that the political entity must stir the popular passions and desire to fight for their political goals through other means, according to the three-step model. This is the only sway they hold over us, their entire military capability – the power to control popular opinion. The establishment will not fight this war with projectiles, it is a war that will be fought with words, i.e. propaganda. Through the might of the pen, the liberal left further their own goals, while seeking to stop us from realizing ours. That is the foremost weapon against us, the one that paralyzes us and keeps us from taking action, for fear of… what? Of becoming outcasts from the collective madness, outcasts from a lemming migration heading for a precipice – is that what keeps us from acting?

Man survives through social acceptance; we are a tribal mammal and we are mutually dependant upon each other. This evolutionary trait has, under normal circumstances, served us well. It is far easier for an individual to break a law written on a piece of paper than it is to break a social norm that renders the individual a social pariah. We will never be able to break free from what we are. We can, however, make clear who belongs to our own tribe, our identity group, our political entity – within which the social norms serve our purpose and promote our way of life. Social acceptance depends wholly on what in-group you belong to. The social blitzkrieg of an enemy group is not just inefficient, but downright pathetic, because it presumes a desire to be included and accepted by the enemy group.

The situation we find ourselves in today is a self-inflicted injury, in that the men and the political establishment have abandoned control of the outer defensive barricades, in favor of fawning before virtue-signaling liberal leftist altruism. A classic counter-measure would be to set up new defensive barricades, not necessarily in a physical sense, within the old ones. This must be done when the enemy is in your midst, and there is a need to isolate yourself from him. It can be achieved through what are commonly termed "cells." If an antagonist talks about the cell, he will often pair it with the word "terror." These cells are created, or rather, arise, due to a decentralized structure, because they are too weak to hold or control a specific geographical area. However, our third-party enemy has accumulated the necessary strength to maintain a more physical defense network via so-called no-go zones. There is a huge difference between controlling a defense mechanism yourself, and having it fall into the hands of your enemy. Normally, the outer line of defense determines whose rules apply within those lines. But our third-party enemy is not a unified political entity. There are constant skirmishes between various Muslim groups as well as other immigrant groups, who have brought ancient tribal conflicts with them to our country. Our enemies make up a myriad of different interests, identities and power struggles.

The no-go zones will have a political impact when they are influential enough to push for exceptions, first on their own behalf; the next step will be to enforce it on others. In the end, sovereignty rests upon your own ability to impose an exception or to uphold it. Once that ability is lost, the unit is no longer the sovereign ruler. That means that if their unit is the sovereign of the area, then we, per definition, are not. The question is – when do we start resisting, thereby starting the war? Remember, war only begins with resistance, which is why the liberal left accuses us of warmongering. And they may well be right – not only do we call for our own defense, we will carry it out. War has an intrinsic tendency to escalate, in line with Clausewitz' ideal war model. Therefore, it is only a matter of time before the resistance, reciprocated by the antagonists, escalates into a *de facto* armed struggle for political and literal survival.

The feminist establishment will always defend attacks committed by "them," and make excuses like "lack of understanding" and "socioeconomic exclusion" – and they will always attack "us" whenever retaliation occurs against the policy and its consequences. We will come under attack, mainly verbally, and be accused of being the reason why "together" does not work – it is our fault, since we oppose it. The same historical revisionism was spouted by these feminized nutjobs in connection with the war in former Yugoslavia, claiming that the war was due to the nationalists, rather than the unsustainable situation that arose due to Balkanization.

Our resistance can and should not only be direct, but also indirect. The resistance should be actively and passively aggressive, by placing us on the outside. Not outside the political conflict, where we are actively aggressive, but outside the control of the liberal left-wing establishment. We all know the nature of the war that is being fought (except the liberal lefties; they have no idea), so there is no need for centralization. In fact, centralization would be harmful. The transition into doing what it takes to achieve what Clausewitz described as the goal of war, to overthrow the enemy, will instead happen directly and be totally adapted to the situation when the anarchic decentralization occurs. All the while the establishment cannot possibly identify the main point that makes it possible for the struggle to continue. This lays the foundation for their fear of us, a fear they do not harbor of the other hostile groups. The reason is of course that there is nothing more frightening than free men – because they are unrestrained, and without limits. We will work inside as well as outside the system at the same time, loyal to our tribe in spirit, loyal to our political unit, where the only social acceptance that matters to us lies. Through our tribes we will challenge the establishment, constantly testing the waters to see how far our authority goes, how much we can get away with – until the dam finally breaks and a new order is implemented.[7]

Most military theorists and analysts today feel that physical capability and combat prowess are not the most important factors to win the battle. It is no longer a soldier's task. This line of reasoning may well be the result of feminization – to emphasize the capacity for violence that the individual soldier has would make the case for female soldiers all the more difficult to argue.

---

[7] For further reading on men's tribal essence, I recommend Jack Donovan's book *How to become a barbarian* (Dissonant Hum, 2016.)

That technological advances have eliminated the need for men's physical dominance seems to be the prevailing train of thought here.

To quote Nassim Taleb, IYI – Intellectual Yet Idiots. The Swedish military cadre of intellectual analysts from the older generation have pretty much all served in the military, in an all-male environment. Their experience and conclusions about military service must therefore have been that it is a job that women could do just as well. The feminized Swedish intelligentsia believes that women are equal to us men, because they themselves feel like they are. What man would enlist in the French Foreign Legion to prove he has what it takes, if it also accepted women?

Denying the man the role of defender means that women can lead the country, make up half the workforce within the military, and chase bad guys in the streets as police officers. IYI completely ignore the capacity for violence. The goal of war is, as I have mentioned before, to overthrow the enemy, yet they assume that this will happen by firing a projectile or manning a drone, far away from front lines – they believe that the war will be fought in front of a computer screen, like playing a video game. They call it RMA – Revolution of Military Affairs, a change so big that it has transformed warfare forever – a total break with the way wars were fought before this so-called revolution. Their analysis has blinded them to the point that they are unable to consider that the future war that is certainly coming may well be fought as much with fists as with bullets. And this is another problem – they have never been in a fistfight. This is the most basic method for a man to get what he wants – by way of the fist. The no-go zones that have been established by our occupying force are not defended by drones, but through brute force. We have lost Swedish territory, places that can no longer be called Swedish other than through illusions *de jure*, without any so-called RMA being involved. Our future war will not be fought in front of a screen – unless you count designing *memes*, writing propaganda and social influence – it will be fought in the past. That which came before linear tactics, operational art and maneuver warfare.

We know what is to come, because we have seen it. When I was in Kiev in Ukraine during the Euromaidan, it was like traveling through time. Not to the fascist era as some would have it, but rather, a bygone era when kings were dethroned and exiled if they were deemed unfit to rule. Battles were fought where both sides used shields and batons; it was a physical struggle that dragged on for months. Both sides had access to handguns, one more than the other, but this was a *coup d'état* that could be carried out through physical dominance. Thanks to their willpower and physical strength, they managed not only to hold on to the territory they had already taken, but to advance to an extent that prompted the then-Prime Minister to flee the country. All thanks to the power of the fist, and some projectiles.

The coup in Turkey in 2016 failed due to the massive gap in the ladder of violence. A tank is not very useful if its only purpose is to be menacing, not actually put to use. That gap did not exist in Ukraine or in National Socialist Germany. Hitler would never have seized power nor been able to hold onto it had it not been for the clenched fist comprised of the SA men. If a political entity wants to implement major changes in society through means other than parliamentarianism, its own potential for violence is far more important than, for example, the support of the military. If the men of the nation are prepared to take to the streets and fight for their own political unit, then it is fair to assume that these men are also prepared to put on uniforms and meet the nation's needs in the armed forces, should the conflict evolve into a full-scale war. This is exactly what happened when the street fighters of the Euromaidan became militiamen by swapping their batons for Kalashnikov rifles, after a need to climb further up the ladder of violence had arisen. The Armed Forces are just the shell of a very blunt, almost obsolete weapon. The man, however, is ever deadly, and what makes the shell come alive.

Thus, the individual potential for violence is important, as every individual is part of a whole. It is not enough to swallow *the red pill* – that only serves to gain an understanding of the situation. It takes more. It takes what Marcus Follin, *The Golden One*, has dubbed "The Glorious Pill." We must build ourselves up to effectively co-ordinate with others and reach a common goal.

The time for "red pills" has passed, the time for glory has come. What separates the two is action. We need a masculine elite that can take back what is rightfully ours. We are men, the greatest beast not only on the planet, but in the entire galaxy – should anything else be out there, that too will be proven through action.

The only way a poodle can get what it wants is to sit still and be submissive. A wolf, on the other hand, has other options. This is the difference between a "friendly" man who act out of necessity, because he is incapable of doing otherwise, and a man who chooses to act this way. The man who chooses friendliness can, if need be, solve his problems without the authority of "the other," he does not need the permission that is the lifeline of the incapable.

If it had been Swedish men rising up and the Euromaidan had played out in Sergels torg of Stockholm, then the scenario would have been quite different, and most certainly would not have lasted for months. The feminized Swedish police force would have had to choose between fleeing, due to the physical balance of power being so off, or staging a massacre by brutally escalating up the ladder of violence. Both options are strategic disasters – a state is nothing if it cannot maintain its monopoly on violence, and the *raison d'être* of our state is implementing and maintaining control – a massacre of its own people would send the opposite signal. Both scenarios played out in Ukraine: the inability to maintain the monopoly on violence, followed by a massacre that spelled the final nail in the coffin for the then-Prime Minister.

To fight a war, one must first establish what kind of war it is, in order to avoid making fatal mistakes. This is the first strategic question that must be answered. The answer tells you what it will take to be victorious. The establishment lacks understanding of war as well as violence, such as the war they are actually in already, and this renders them incapable of formulating a strategy that could bring them victory. War is always waged in order to achieve a specific goal. Instead, they will try to compensate for the lack of a correct problem analysis with increased tactical and operative force. In other words, try to treat the symptoms instead of doing the right thing, which in this case would be to euthanize the dying patient.

Regardless of who wins, the democratic experiment as we know it – including the influence of females – will only have survived for about 100 years. By default, the experiment was doomed to failure before it even got started. It was never a question of if the system would collapse, but when. To have men rule is no guarantee for success, but to have women dominate society is, on the other hand, a certain road to socialism and misery. Public life is simply not their domain, and cannot be dealt with in the same manner as private life.

The parliamentary failure of the 20th century to eliminate the "us" for the benefit of "them", under the pretence that this creates commonality and a state of being "together", will echo into the future as the worst example of failed statesmanship ever. Changes will have to be made at the expense of what we now know as women's rights; that is, primarily female political influence, e.g. voting rights, multiculturalism, along with all kinds of leftist political theory-crafting such as feminism, social constructivism, socialism, communism, leftist liberalism and so on.

THE STATE

*A state, is called the coldest of all cold monsters.
Coldly lieth it also; and this lie creepeth from
its mouth: "I, the state, am the people."* –
Nietzsche

Political Science defines the state as the organization
that has complete control over a fixed geographical
area. Complete control is ensured through the state's
monopoly on violence. It guarantees that no other
party can enforce its will through means other than
those permitted by law within the boundaries of the
outer defenses that make up the nation's geographical
borders. A monopoly on violence is not just a necessity
for the state to function, it is the very definition of it.

Our founding father Gustav Vasa institutionalized the
monopoly on violence in Sweden. When he disarmed
the bishop's guards, the state became the only party that
could initiate violence *de jure*. This meant that the state
of Sweden could practice violence within the realm,
without any consideration for local power elites.

The state as we know it was supposedly born because

the state power grew tired of all the violence, and realized that order could only be restored through the implementation of Leviathan. People were killing each other left and right, and the state had to put its foot down and tell them to stop – or taste the wrath and violence of the state. This is nothing but a government propaganda myth – a self-deceiving lie to justify our submission. The monopoly on violence was implemented to disarm any threats to the sovereign power of the ruler – not to prevent a "war of all against all."

To uphold the new power structure, a standing army was required, a threshold effect that ensured "the order", in this case government control of the monopoly on violence, and made sure the subjects abided by it. The reorganization implemented by Gustav Vasa also gave birth to the Swedish navy – initially mercenaries hired from Lübeck on credit, to fight the Danish logistics line blocking occupied Stockholm. In fact, the troops were retained without any payment being made. Lübeck, however, lacked the military strength to reclaim that which had been lost through this blatant breach of contract.

A standing police/military force (back then more often than not the same thing) required organizational development and institutional changes. Resources needed to be allocated and coordinated. As is the case in modern times, it was expensive to recruit and arm a professional force. That laid the groundwork for the rise of the absolute state, which would later, by gaining total control, also gain the ability to reorganize society as a whole. When the state became absolute, so of necessity did the wars.

Along with other European countries, the Swedish tax state – also sometimes referred to as the military state – evolved as a major part of state finances were dedicated to the Armed Forces. One country's military capabilities needed to be matched by the other countries that were within reach of a possible act of violence. A phenomenon now known as a security dilemma. Until the 19th century, and the breakthrough of capitalism, 90 percent of Swedish taxes went to the Armed Forces.

The state is a modern invention in human history. The state did not give birth to Sweden, Mother Svea is much older and nobler than that. Sweden is our place on earth, the co-existence between the land and its people, the domain where the Swedes thrive, provided that we can defend the symbiosis that is Sweden. The state, on the other hand, is a tool, an instrument that helps realize the authority of the sovereign. The state of Sweden was born to serve a purpose, and that purpose was to streamline the implementation of Gustav Vasa's will.

Throughout the ages, every authority has used a specific methodology in order to enforce its rule. The big difference between then and now, and the formation of the state that came to constitute the modern country, is that the latter has come to have a life of its own. What used to be a tool to manage the system, a means to an end, has now become an end in itself, a machine that we are now forced to serve. And it is not just the people that are servants to the state, even the "leaders" are its subordinates. Frederick the Great said: *"Ein Fürst ist der erste Diener seines Staates"*[1], a prince is the first servant of his state. A pretty non-Machiavellian view of statesmanship.

---

[1] Frederick II's response to Machiavelli's *The Prince, Anti-Machiavel*, see chapter 1, "What a strong prince really is, and how one can reach that point."

We are the servants of the state, and the state will have it no other way. It has become the organizational equivalent of the movie The Terminator – where A.I. (Artificial Intelligence) is created to serve man, but instead decides to live by its own rules, completely ignoring the wishes of those it was meant to serve.

The state is its own persona, a separate identity that has emerged from something that used to be dead and abstract. It is Frankenstein's monster. A horrifying walking corpse that lives, according to the Hobbesian political philosophy, to obtain control and security for mankind through its hideous and terrifying appearance, a creature that no one dares defy.

It is an organizational form that has come to dominate our way of thinking, to the degree that we are unable to think outside its existence. However, it exists only in our minds, and is realized through our words and actions. Independent and separate from man, it is no more real than fairy tales. Thus, the state has truly replaced theology. Belief in the state is the great superstition of our time, and what keeps us from greatness. The repressive force that makes true freedom impossible. A mental ball and chain that gains physical control through the state-worshipping fellow man that submits to and worships the state monster. Then and now, to question God meant severe negative consequences – implemented by those who followed God's teachings, not by God himself.

We obtained our state under the pretense that it would entail domestic control, a security that would protect us from arbitrary use of violence. The latter was formulated as a social contract – we submit, but in turn we get to live safe lives. The state also attempted to gain external control through the Westphalian Peace Treaty, where states are formally recognized as the only legitimate entity with which to negotiate war and peace. In reality, this meant that the complete monopoly on violence was implemented not just internally in Sweden, but also externally through the formation of a state cartel, which collectively became the only parties that could declare and wage war.

This has changed our view of war, into a state operation rather than a human one. We hide behind the monster. The importance of the state has also been reinforced by the most important military theorist of our time, Carl von Clausewitz, who described war as an extension of politics by other means. Clausewitz divided war into a trinity, made up of the people, the military commander and the political leaders of the state. It lays the groundwork for the symmetry one expects in war – if it is waged between states. If the trinity is not in place, an asymmetry is created, the most important component when it comes to surprising your antagonist with unforeseen, unplanned events. Without a legitimate counterpart, the war is considered a police matter, a force whose job it is to establish and maintain an acceptable order. In the West today, this is known as "nation-building", mainly in the Middle East, where our war efforts can be described as some kind of extreme nation castigation – "you need to beat some sense into certain people."

The state, in other words, becomes the only legitimate party that can dispense violence internally as well as externally. The only keeper of law and order that the states themselves accept. The administration of justice must be done through state-sanctioned channels.

There has not been a single attempt to implement a constitutional restriction that limits the absolute power of the state, a distribution of power, *check and balance*, to the only thing that the state cannot do without – the monopoly on violence, is being the only entity that has the definitive final word when it comes to right and wrong, and through its superior potential for violence, its ability to implement what is *right* without friction. With all facts on hand, it has turned out that the constitution is not enough when it comes to constraining the growth of the dreadful creature that is the state. The United States started out with the smallest state apparatus in the world, a seemingly perfect little creation, where the *Founding Fathers* were well aware that they had created a beast and realized that it needed to be harnessed with the strongest chains available. Like Tyr and the Aesir, they believed they could restrain the wolf Fenrir, to ensure the security of mankind. But as it turned out, nothing could keep Fenrir from breaking loose and destroying the world in Ragnarok.

The state is an entity that, if unrestrained, is an absolute, it is the central power base within a set geographical area, one that no other entity can dominate or even oppose. To compromise with another political entity is to limit your own leeway – an unacceptable act to the state. For that reason, it was poetically beautiful to witness the political struggle that unfolded at Bundy ranch in 2014. It showed the innermost essence of politics, which consists solely of the most basic means of male communication – the ability to convey your will through other means than verbalizing, through action and a clenched fist.

What happened at Bundy Ranch differed significantly from what the left-wingers display through violent confrontation and infantile protests. The left does not challenge the monopoly on violence of the state, they add to it. They are the female counterpart, trying to get the state to hit on their behalf through hysterical outbursts.

The federal authority, the Bureau of Land Management (BLM), wanted to charge Cliven Bundy a fee, based on the grazing rights of his livestock. Bundy declared that he did not recognize the authority of the BLM over his livestock or their pasture land, and refused to pay the fee. This resulted in armed federal agents being sent out to the Bundy Ranch, to impound his livestock. Because this was considered by them a non-constitutional act by the federal authority, a number of militias gathered to defend Bundy, among them, the Oath Keepers, the White Mountain Militia and the Praetorian Guard. This was no longer just about the livestock or the Bundy Ranch, and Bundy himself told Fox News: "This is a lot bigger deal than just my cows. It's a statement for freedom and liberty and the Constitution."[2]

What followed was a two-day deadlock, where hundreds of armed militiamen and federal agents stared each other down, with snipers on both sides. Between the militia and the federal agents, there were the state police and the sheriff, trying to maintain order by mediating between the two groups. Eventually, the BLM backed down and released the livestock that had been impounded, announcing that they would seek other administrative and legal means of exerting

---

[2] Hernandez & Langdon (2014) *The Guardian* [online] "Federal rangers face off against armed protesters in Nevada 'range war'" https://www.theguardian.com/world/2014/apr/13/nevada-bundy-cattle-ranch-armed-protesters [Accessed 22 Aug. 2017]

pressure in order to collect the fee they had demanded. As I write this, in 2017, the dispute has still not been resolved.

Freedom works like a muscle – if it is not exercised and strengthened through resistance, it will atrophy. Something that is supposed to be strong, functional and aesthetically desirable, instead becomes decrepit, weak and disgustingly incapable of maintaining itself. The latter is the state-hugger, who cannot see how he would survive if not for the regulations and subsidies of the state. Herein lies the big difference between how the concept of freedom is perceived in Europe *vis-à-vis* the United States. What has become known as negative versus positive freedom, where negative freedom means the freedom of action that is made possible in an environment without constraints and prohibitions, and positive freedom means that the citizen has a chance to act, but at the expense of others due to redistribution policies. An American tradition that hails from John Locke, and a European one from Jean-Jacques Rousseau, the practices of which evolved into a legacy from the American and French revolutions.

That is the big difference between these two revolutions, each claiming to fight for freedom, but clearly defining the concept in different ways.

The American colonists sought to govern themselves, because they did not feel a need to have a faraway king in London rule over them. This was the emphasis of their struggle, and they had no intention of swapping one tyrant for another. The autonomy would, as far as possible, reach all the way down to the individual level. The God-given right to life, liberty and property was the guiding principle, later included in the Constitution as the entire *raison d'être* of the state. Thus, the state became the guarantor when it came to upholding these God-given rights. The distribution of power stipulated in the Constitution became the chains that held the state in check, preventing tyranny and ensuring individual freedom rights in the pursuit of life, liberty and happiness.

The French constitution today still talks about *liberté, égalité et fraternité* – freedom, equality and brotherhood, the slogans of the French revolution. That fight was not about breaking the chains of the masters within the monarchy, it was about replacing them with themselves – the people. They replaced the tyranny of the monarchy with the tyranny of the people. Everyone would get the same opportunities, and by abolishing the privileged class, everyone would become privileged – but a privilege always exists at the expense of something else; it is a right based on anything *except merit*.

When the people appoint themselves the privileged class, and at the same time demand to be funded by the people because no distinction is made, it is the equivalent of a snake trying to feed itself by swallowing its own tail. A way of thinking and a concept of freedom that has been prevalent in Social Democratic Sweden, dominating all political life regardless of party affiliations – everyone on board, no one left behind. However, the true meaning of this credo is that no one should be able to leave the fold, and use their individual prowess to excel and get ahead – everyone is devoured by the collective and united by the lowest common denominator to implement an artificial equality. It contradicts the only concept of freedom worthy of the name, negative freedom; free men are not equal and equal men are not free. The people of France, and other places inspired by the revolution, never sought to free the people. They simply wanted to elevate the people to a position of power, where they could devour themselves through the beneficial, self-serving concept of freedom, brotherhood and equality.

The United States is far from perfect, but it is the only real attempt in modern times to limit the state's influence via the Constitution, and the American Revolution strove to give men the freedom to act according to their own judgment and bear the consequences of their decisions themselves. A state of high moral standards, which does not want to enslave its people, but rather, rule with their consent. And if the state becomes tyrannical and the consent between the citizens and the state ceases, the moral right to overthrow the government by bearing arms and forming militias is right there, in the United States Constitution.

The American governmental apparatus is meant to be an instrument that protects life, liberty and property, based on the rule of law. The law is supposed to be the authority, not a tool for implementing either the will of the sovereign or the will of the people, no matter what case is made for the abstract "greater good." Executive power should only be exercised within the confines of what the law allows, while the actions of the citizen are only limited by what is legally prohibited. *Might* is effectively subordinate to *Right*.

Despite all this, the American state has grown into a welfare monster, more along the lines of the European concept of freedom than what the United States Constitution originally intended. The United States Constitution has thereby either allowed the growth of the American state, or been unable to stop it. To use an analogy: If a person does not follow the job description, and delivers the opposite result of what he is employed to do, then this person is not likely to be promoted by the company he works for.

The question is if we will be able to reset the American state and get back to constitutional principles, thereby gaining a new opportunity *to create a* new, enduring polity based on freedom. A new attempt at breaking away from the American federation by some states is not an unlikely scenario. Or maybe our best chance is breaking new terrain in the cosmos, thereby rendering the existence of the United States less important. The colonization would of course have to be done as a state enterprise, alternatively by cutting the umbilical cord to the state and allowing a private or co-operatively owned company explore and populate the unknown. It is unlikely that this will happen in Europe, though, since we, the right-wing opposition, do not primarily seek to free ourselves, but rather, to replace the captain and first mate.

One of the more obvious measures to prevent the state from growing, making the private public, is by repealing the 19th Amendment of the Constitution, which has turned out to be devastating to minimal state formation.[3] What was once self-evident did not need to be discussed, since a discussion is the antithesis of

---

[3] For further reading on the subject of the connection between women's suffrage and the expansion of the state, I refer mainly to the scientific article "Did Women's Suffrage Change the Size and Scope of Government?" by John R. Lott of Yale University, and Lawrence W. Kenny of the University of Florida, but also to my book *Handen som gungar vaggan* (2015).

the obvious. Obvious things were unwritten norms that later became institutionalized and thereby regulated to become doable, but times change and new circumstances arise when old threats disappear, paving the way for a new dynamic in society. The lack of clear threats and the creation of a safe environment dampens the societal need for strict gender roles. In a cross cultural study, the anthropologist Gilmore found that constant calm, peace and abundant resources create a window for feminism. The system of gender roles, unwritten as well as written, that has been the foundation of our evolutionary survival, is now in question and said to be an artificial power construction that has allowed men to retain a privileged position through social reconstruction.

However, the thing that the leftists, feminists and in particular the Social Justice Warriors point to as an artificial societal construction to keep men in power has actually been instrumental when it comes to solving a *problem* we have forgotten about today. The elimination of what they view as *oppression* will remind us of this problem, because it will invariably return once its solution has been removed. Their propagandizing for the norm-breaking society will bring dire consequences – and the doom of our civilization, should they succeed. Social constructivism views man as moldable, and through the power of the state, equality – which in their deluded minds is the same as justice – can be achieved. For this reason, the state must be all-consuming, and the two parties thrive in their interaction, at the expense of our freedom and in the long run, our survival.

Societal norms serve to uphold, defend or strengthen what we are; that is the basis for consistency. It has been of the utmost importance to every society to control and channel male aggression, but to control female sexuality has been even more important. A defective normative behavior from the former would not necessarily spell doom, it would just result in a savage society; whereas the latter would unavoidably lead to a decay that would be very hard to recover from.

We, the sexes, are two different beings and a society with its culture is an extension of who we are. If the culture changes into something that we cannot sustain, based solely on what the social constructionists *want it to be*, then that society will perish – by the cold hand of time or by being driven out by another political entity that draws power from practice instead of ideology. A society cannot possibly survive either sluts or cowards. If you, when reading this, automatically categorized sluts as women and cowards as men that means you still have a functioning, culturally normative mind, and have not fallen for the social constructivists' propaganda.

In order to survive over time, not just physically but also still in control of our own unit as a competitive entity compared to other units whose life force seeks the ever-present conflict, the struggle for dominion, it is essential to view life within the unit from an administrative point of view. Administration is about transference, and in society this happens fluidly between generations. Society's collective resources, the purpose of which is to ensure the continued dominance of the political unit, are not handed over to a new generation at a certain point in time; the transference is constant and literally happening all the time. This knowledge is what prompted Aristotle to object vigorously to Plato's "ideal republic."[4]

---

[4] See Aristoteles *The politics*, book II.

To make a respectful and constructive transference possible, a natural affection for the up-and-coming generation is required. The love of one's own, the people who will replace our generation, the same way that we replaced those who came before us, those who labored with blood, sweat and tears, lovingly, for our sake. A legacy that becomes stronger with each passing generation. All because we love our own kin and wish them all the best – and we are prepared to bleed to make sure that what they inherit is worth something. A man does not labor for someone else's family, he labors for the well-being of his own family. That is the primary thing, but any surplus may well go to the extended family, in order to create prosperity for all, and strengthen the in-group vis-à-vis other groups. To realize this, it takes what Aristotle describes as the natural affection for one's own, an affection that is not possible in Plato's Republic. Plato believed that the women should serve "the greater good of society," through a eugenic government program, scrapping the idea of marriage as well as monogamy. Any offspring would be raised by the Republic – for the Republic. Thus, no one would know whose children they are except the government, which would mean that the men would labor for someone else's family rather than their own family. Death for the natural affection for your own next of kin. The loving face of society would exclusively come from the cold institution of government, where love of all means love of no one. This illustrates the difference between the cohesion of the family and that which exists in a municipal orphanage.

It is *ipso facto* only the woman that can say with certainty that the child is hers. A societal promotion and acceptance of female promiscuity yields a fatherless and cold society. Families become composed of bastards, which the man is either aware of, and as a true cuckservative he introduces them as his wife's children, belonging to the wife's former or current boyfriend; alternatively, the man is unaware that he has a young cuckoo in the nest. Regardless of which, the respectful transference of societal administration to the next generation will cease, to the detriment of the political in-group. In his book *Sex and Culture*, the anthropologist Joseph Daniel Unwin (1895-1936), Oxford & Cambridge University, presented the thesis that the growth of a civilization is directly related to the chastity of its women.

Before decadence took over and society began to crumble, sexual virtue was of the utmost importance to Greek and Roman women. This normative rule maintained women's honor as well as societal well-being through family formation. To the men, virtue was instead proven through *andreia* and *virtus* – a good male character based on courage and valor. Male virtue, unlike the female version, was based on action – a means to an end. The biological *raison d'être* of women is connected to pregnancy. A woman may well question whether she has really fulfilled her role as a woman if she never experiences the essence of what it means to be a woman, that is, realize her purpose by becoming a mother. It is comparable to the way in which a man may question his view of himself *as a man* if he has never shown courage and mental stamina on the battlefield, shielding his tribe through action. A coward would passively stand aside if war came knocking on his door, leaving his family defenseless and at the mercy of the attacker. A man's honor is directly linked to his willingness to fight. It is so deeply ingrained in us that war has become a direct consequence of our very existence.

There is only one way for a man to prove that he is not a coward, an honorless coward that cannot defend himself, let alone others, and that is by daring, and daring is doing. It becomes a dare, a challenge that may well result in the death of one party in the confrontation that follows an accusation intended to de-masculinize the opponent. It is the ultimate way to show courage – by risking your life. Because that is what is required of the man, in order to defend himself and his loved ones in a life-threatening situation. And it is not just his life at stake in the physical fight; it is the lives of everyone who depends on his capability to win that fight. A woman, on the other hand, would not be insulted if someone called her a coward; that would be considered a very strange insult, and she would most likely just shake her head at it. Her survival and well-being in the tribe do not depend on her courage. She is more vulnerable to insults connected to sexual behavior, such as being called a slut or whore.

Loose women are a great expense to society, the same way cowardly men are.

Therefore there is an organizational purpose to the co-ordination of the tribe – to uphold norms in order to create the beneficial conditions necessary to survive. The prevailing culture can either dampen or amplify what nature intended, but it can never transform us into something we are not. Men's *joie de vivre* lies in the competitive battle lust, and depending on how the norm in society fans those flames, they will flare up into a burning inferno, or be stifled and reduced to nothing but an idea, a dream of something that could one day come true. If there is no fire, the deadly cold will in time come creeping in. However, the fire that keeps you comfortably warm can also burn you, if left unchecked. The intensity of the fire is pivotal to well-being as well as misery.

The societal factors that control normative intensity depend on the tribe's need for men who are willing to fight. If there is no threat against the in-group, then the men are not just unnecessary – they may even be perceived as a danger to society, people who may disturb the peace. If so, they will not be celebrated as the pillars of the community that they actually are, but instead be viewed with some skepticism. This creates a dysgenic negative interaction between the sexes, because natural selection is displaced, from the fundamental masculine objective of keeping society safe to focusing on gaining high status within the safe structure. Men do not fight just to protect their women, but also to make themselves attractive to women. No woman in need will want a coward for a husband. If no need or threat is at hand, the man does not have to fight to defend women or to attract them, instead, he will develop other strategies to achieve this. These strategies may well be a detriment to society, should another threat arise. And, as Aristotle pointed out, quite correctly, we are the things we repetedly do. This is what defines us – our actions, not our words. If we cannot even fight against each other under ritualized conditions, how are we supposed to fight in an environment that has no rules?

A great example of the pre-state phenomenon of distribution of violence, before the implementation of monopoly on violence, may be observed in the two football hooligan groups of Stockholm, AIK and Djurgården, who love to clash on as well as off the football field. They resemble a kind of modern hoplites, lining up in phalanx, with a set number of men, in a particular location, at a particular time, to measure their strength against the other group, following a number of set rules. But like the old hoplites, a distinction is made between inner and outer enemies, the ones that belonged to the Greek civilization and the ones that did not. Hoplites from the various city-states came together to defend against Xerxes II and his approaching Persian army, to defend the freedom of the Greek civilization. This of course happened without any exchange of polite phrases and without clarifying any rules of battle, or when and where it would take place. The same methodology and distinctions were applied in 2016, when the two groups performed a joint physical attack against the consequences of the immigration policy, which received international media attention.[5]

This was not an acceptable civic initiative to the government, because it challenged the sovereign power of the state. The state decides whether something should take place outside of normal procedure, regulated

---

[5] Following a perceived increase in crime at the Stockholm Central Station, the two hooligan groups chose to declare the social contract void, replace submission with security and act directly against the alleged offenders. Andersson & Willgress (2016-01-31) *Daily Mail* [online] "Inside the Neo-Nazi 'firm': Swedish football hooligans tell how they teamed up to launch vicious attack on Stockholm migrants". Available at: http://www.dailymail.co.uk/news/article-3425299/Inside-Neo-Nazi-firm-Swedish-football-hooligans-tell-teamed-launch-vicious-attack-Stockholm-migrants.html [Accessed 22 Aug. 2017]

by law, and the state implements that exception within its own organization, citing the importance of maintaining control as the reason. However, if a state lacks the strength or the will, and is therefore unable to make a decision about such an exception when faced with an opponent that does not follow the rules, the right of sovereignty expires.

The only internal force that can threaten the sovereign is the men, and in the absence of an external threat, the sovereign will de-masculinize men as a safety precaution. In the extreme case of Sweden, the process has gone even further. Here, the characteristic male expressions are not just dampened, but annihilated in an attempt to feminize the men – and make them equal to women. Gender does not exist, other than as a social construct. Through the welfare state and the dominant feminine liberal leftist ideology, society has tried to institutionalize the men away. Instead, the state offers that which has always been offered by men; that is, security and a livelihood. Before the state came into play, this was regulated according to the principal of "give something, get something," but now, it is viewed as a political right – you do not have to offer anything of value in order to get protection, thus generating a net cost that someone else has to balance. This is a Marxist transaction, and as such, it will not stand the test of time.

A double-edged sword has been swung against masculinity. The lack of war and external threats has made war games, designed to demonstrate the men's prowess in battle and their willingness to risk their lives, obsolete. The other edge is the state's need for total control, a control that in the end rests on the ability to enforce the law. The latter is the antithesis of men taking the law into their own hands, and the direct consequence is that the government subsidizes and protects the culprit, when it prevents any kind of civic retribution, regardless of the crime. But that is not all. The state also prevents free men from administering their own justice between themselves, i.e. in single combat, because it would mean transferring the legal decision about what is *right* from the state to free men, and that would strip the almighty lawmaker of his power.

Single combat would, for instance, put a stop to false accusations, thereby tempering the effect of any litigation that followed.

In a dispute, both parties would have to back up their claims and demands with their lives. The sword is a more credible alternative than mere words in a dispute based only on hearsay. Action is the only glorious alternative to petty squabbles.

To fight becomes, and is, a natural part of the legal process, deeply rooted in a Germanic custom going all the way back to the first written texts about the Germanic peoples, up until late modern times, before the domestication of men via the devastating civilization process took off in the 20th century. To defend your honor, weapon in hand, to fight to spill your own blood as well as that of your antagonist, becomes crucial to maintain and clarify to others that words have a price tag attached to them. To speak is a right inherent in liberty, but like all other rights it can only be preserved if someone is ready to fight for it, by putting up a fight himself, or getting somebody else to fight on his behalf. The state now decides what can and cannot be said. Freedom of speech has gone from being every man's right to something the masses allow you out of their mercy.

National Socialist Germany reinstated the legal duel in the 1930s, rendering it inside and outside the law at the same time. Inside, because it was regulated by law, outside because it dictated the legal verdict itself. Duels were massively popular in Austria. One of the best known Austrian fighters of the time was commando Otto Skorzeny,[6] later dubbed "Scarface" by the allied forces, due to a large scar on his face, which he obtained while dueling in college. The scar remains the silent glory. The honorable testimony to the willingness of the individual to stand up for himself, and dedicate himself in combat for the sake of his loved ones, if necessary. Thus, duels also served a purpose in the German war system, as it is the ultimate action a civilian can take to prove he is prepared to kill and be killed. Both are essential to the war capability, and the ritualized violence that the duel offers ensures that the people are prepared to look beyond their own lives.

Before the feminization of the American legal system, duels were not only allowed, they were a matter of course, not just in the "Wild West", but also in the industrialized and "civilized" eastern United States. Even members of the government solved their own conflicts by themselves, among them Vice President Aaron Burr versus former Treasury Secretary Alexander Hamilton, in 1804. President Andrew Jackson, one of the founders of the Democratic Party, had a number of duels on his record when he took office. One was against the

---

[6] Skorzeny became notorious after the successful rescue of Mussolini in 1943. He was known as Hitler's boldest soldier, and later as the most dangerous man in Europe. See Skorzeny, Otto (2011), *Skorzeny's Special Missions: The Memoirs of Hitler's Most Daring Commando*, Zenith Press.

governor of Tennessee, when Jackson himself was the highest military commander of the Tennessee militia. 30 American states still to this day remain faithful to the Constitution, in that they have not outlawed duels *per se*.[7] However, the victor in a duel will be found guilty of either murder or grievous bodily harm, depending on the outcome. The legal mandate therefore lies with the individual states and the federal government.

In the West, duels were viewed as a natural way to handle injustices right up until the end of the 19th century. The duel was a solution to a dispute, where the participants literally risked their lives. At the same time, the rest of society was spared any involvement. So, it is not just the participants taking the legal decision out of the hands of society; they also make sure that society is not dragged into the conflict, by making sure it does not evolve into a family feud, something that could become a catalyst for outright civil war.

There were a number of attempts to prohibit the independent justice of the citizens, but as it turned out, it was hard for the pubescent state monster to implement and maintain order. The state had not yet grown into its complete, absolute condition, where it could control society as a whole. Great Britain led the way, and banned dueling on a permanent basis in 1841.

When dueling was banned, only sports remained as a civilian preparation for armed and deadly combat. Violence has a twofold perspective – men fight to kill, and men fight to avoid killing. Sports connected with the war system are very different from the duel, since

---

[7] Van Creveld, Martin (2013). *Wargames from gladiators to gigabytes,* Cambridge University Press, p. 131.

they take place in the form of practice and contest, not as a part of the legal process. In the ritualized violence of sports, war becomes peace and serenity for all to enjoy. This is very unlike the duel as well as war, which are both fought for the purpose of attaining a peaceful agreement. If the government represses this peacekeeping activity, this possibility of letting off steam, the underlying factors that generate war will start to boil under the surface without any outlet.

Football (soccer) has, for example, existed in many different forms throughout the ages. In days of yore, it was not uncommon that matches had a deadly outcome. Not by design, but as an accepted part of the sport's positive side effects – if the purpose was to prepare for war. Now, imagine who you would like to have in your platoon on a hostile raid, or defending against one – an Italian football team or a rugby team from New Zealand. I will leave you to ponder that thought without further comment. Okay, I cannot resist, I will make one comment. European football has been feminized to a degree where we celebrate sissies, who fake injury just to get a free kick, like heroes – the antithesis of what a hero originally was. In the best of worlds, the local football team or its hooligan followers would form the local militia. They would turn sports into war again. The connection that has always been there would once again be realized.

So, after prohibiting men from dispensing their own internal justice, sports were feminized too. And now, we can surely say that for the first time in history, the western man is not free to spill his own as well as his opponent's blood to the last drop. Any kind of antagonistic battle that means the participants risk losing their lives has been outlawed, or regulated beyond recognition. The man has become the great anachronism of our age, and the state, motivated by self-interest, seeks to subdue the men into becoming like the docile women. There is a utopian desire to uphold the law by a seemingly impartial objective entity – the foundation of the rule of law, with emphasis on a universal equality before the law. People are aware enough, and intellectual enough, to understand that if a crime is committed against an innocent victim, it might be them next time if nothing is done. The effect of the rule of law is that it confuses crimes against innocent people with the righteous act of a free man that exacts justice for himself and his kin – the difference between murder and rightful removal. And this is precisely the point of the law. Free men today are without rights, when their grievances and injustices are pushed aside. It is only when these men take action against the injustice that the law really gets involved, and the state exacts revenge against anyone who dares challenge the lawmaker's authority.

The reason that we do not kill our neighbor has nothing to do with the government's superior capacity for violence; the reason may be found elsewhere. However, it does play a part in why we do not kill our neighbor when he actually deserves it, or at least force him to leave the area, one way or another. A justice system like that was the reason the Vikings became the first Europeans to set foot on Greenland as well as on the North American mainland.

Erik the Red was "asked" to leave Iceland, after having killed a local man in a brawl. The Icelanders did not care where he went, as long as he did not stay in Iceland. In other words, it did not matter if he went to Hel or took to the seas – the important thing was the end result, that

Erik could not harm another Icelander. Because Erik and his father Torvald had already been asked to leave Norway after a similar incident, Erik decided to go west instead. He made history as the discoverer of Greenland in 982, consolidating the image of the Vikings as explorers and challengers of the unknown. Erik the Red's son, Leif Eriksson, went on to travel even further west, and became the first European to establish a settlement in *Vinland*, now known as North America.[8]

Before the tax state emerged, the legal system was simplified and natural – to lock up and isolate unwanted individuals was considered unnecessary and wasteful. The few times it happened, it was due to political power games within the aristocracy, and the purpose was not primarily to mete out justice.

If someone has committed a crime serious enough that the people of that society deem him unfit to be among them, it is the most natural thing in the world to remove him. Depending on the nature of the crime, the punishment should be enforced either by outlawing the person, thereby carrying it out implicitly if no one is prepared to defend him, or via single combat if the crime is an unforgivable wrongdoing against an individual. Even at lower levels of injustice, if society could not accept having the person as a neighbor, he was forced to leave the specific geographical area. Where he went was totally insignificant, the only relevant point was that he did not stick around to keep pestering his neighbors. A society that is not afraid of conflict can "ask" its denizens to leave and never return, which sets

---

[8] For further reading, see the *Saga of Erik the Red*, and the *Greenland Saga*, from the *Sagas of Icelanders*.

a healthy precedent for strangers aspiring to integrate into the in-group.

The possibility of infighting serves the essential purpose of keeping one's own political unit strong, in a natural eugenic sense. Those who are capable of fighting each other also develop their joint battle capability. Internal skirmishes, single combat and blood sports are nothing if not preparatory war games, to hone the skills and courage needed when faced with an external enemy. Losing such a battle is only possible if you do not participate. Glory can never be attained without activity. Thus, to be the losing party does not mean a loss *per se*, because at the very least, the participant has shown that he is not a coward. He is prepared to fight the good fight, prepared to take action when insulted.

We are forbidden to fight amongst ourselves – to hone the skills nature has bestowed upon us, traits that are the very definition of what we are. The state's monopoly on violence makes sure there is no infighting, because that would be a threat to the centralized control. Not that long ago, civilian marksmen and the Armed Forces actually cooperated in Sweden. Of course, that was before the state started to view its own citizens as potential enemies, and a larger threat to its own sovereignty than the surrounding states.

The fateful process of civilizing society has left no room for the essence of men. Man is to be tamed to fit the so-called civilization, on the pretext that he will otherwise become a threat to the same. A slow transformation from wolf to lapdog. The warrior's world is very different from the civilian world he protects. It is realism versus liberalism. It is power politics versus love, care and understanding. The warrior is in complete symbiosis with the civilian life. If there is no civilian life for the warrior to defend, then the warrior/ man is nothing but a destructive force. If, on the other hand, the warrior is not there for the civilians, they will soon be faced with that same destructive force.

The man has a foot in both worlds, he is part of the outer perimeter as well as the civilian life. These two roles are diametrically opposed. While the first benefits from unbridled and hostile aggression, the latter would be severely damaged by it. It all rests on the man's understanding of the political, who belongs to his in-group, the civilian part of the political unit that has to be defended, and who are "the others," the political unit whose interests collides with his, and therefore must be fought violently. The two roles are two separate beings, the masculine warrior and the feminine civilian – they do not speak the same language, nor do they view the world through the same lens.

What the warrior does to his enemy, who represents the other interest group and therefore another political unit, is not what a warrior does within his own political unit. The former, depending on the distance between the units, has fewer rules the further away from each other the groups are, until no rules apply. That is the state of absolute political enmity, where anything goes. However, if a warrior has that attitude towards his own political unit in order to promote his own personal interests, he becomes a person against whom society must protect itself, and the warrior needs to be removed for good, since he is clearly incapable of separating friend from foe. That would be the reverse pattern of our leftist, feminist, liberal society, where everybody is friends and enemies do not exist – no friends, only enemies. Both types wreak havoc on the in-group.

Today, male aggression in the civilian community is kept in check through the total monopoly on violence, which aims to disarm our essence as men. It is a spiritual castration of our masculinity, and it leaves no effective outlet for our aggression. Instead of the monopoly on violence as a centralized control, aggression should be kept in check through a completely decentralized apparatus of violence, absolutely anarchic, resulting in a necessary power distribution, check and balance, in the use of violence. Applied to politics, this is a beautiful thing, because it makes politics more real. There are no longer any illusions as to what is going on. Politics is what happens when different interests collide – the question as to how and what is the best solution to the unavoidable conflict that comes from the collision. Politics is realized through the decision, leading to the submission of one party, or mutual negotiation. The latter can sometimes happen via the ballot box, to avoid unnecessary bloodshed, but sometimes weapons, violence, and threat of violence, are the only means available to prevent an escalation of the political enmity. Violently resisting a political decision can sometimes be a good way to prevent an escalation that will damage society – by setting small fires to clear the deadwood, a huge wildfire is prevented. The act of physical resistance shows the other side that trying to impose their will on the enemy will be more costly to them, than a revolution or war would be to the party that will not submit. Domestic policy is the proxy of civil war – seeking a peaceful solution that all conflicting parties may find acceptable, via the parliamentary system. If, on the other hand, the solution is not acceptable to a political entity, the political process may instead become a catalyst for something lethal. However, a political entity that has no storm troopers, men who are prepared to give their lives for politics, is not a unit to be reckoned with.

To push a political enemy too far may be counterproductive, if he has the power to discontinue the political interaction and move forward by other means, as Clausewitz puts it. It can be equally devastating not to push your political enemy at all. He will then get a window of opportunity to gain influence over your political unit, possibly with deadly consequences as it is at the mercy of the other, if you cannot strike back when pushed. In other words – too much violence against a political enemy is just as harmful to you as too little.

We need a political system that does not aspire to Kant's *Perpetual Peace*[9], but aims to bring society back into its natural state of *Perpetual Threat* – not too high, but not too low – Aristotle's golden mean that cuts through two extremes. A safe society that knows that *de facto* comes before *de jure*. A society that does not point the finger at masculine culture as the root of all insecurities, because it knows that in a lawless society, masculinity is the root of safety and security, and the foundation of all societal development.

By dissolving the monopoly on violence, *Might* is once again subordinated to *Right*, as it in practice means a return to having to consider the will of local power elites, making it more difficult to use politics as coercion. It would actually make it impossible for politicians to act against the interests of local people, without risking

---

[9] See Immanuel Kant's philosophic essay from 1795; *Perpetual Peace*.

serious friction. This would be a decentralized and local phenomenon, in line with the MAD (Mutual Assured Destruction) doctrine. The benefits of all political decisions implemented against the will of the people would have to be carefully weighed against the risk of potential uprisings.

The abolition of the monopoly on violence would mean that the sovereign leader of the society would have to act within the frames of compromise that the people find acceptable. Through constant negotiation, the principle of trading something of value for something else is assured. A leader, formal or informal, has nothing to fear from his own people, unless he unleashes the storm by demanding something unreasonable from those he claims to represent. A decentralized and anarchic system will mean that an unjust leader will run the risk of getting a noose tied around his neck in a more literal way. It will be a return to our tradition and history – free men are capable of bearing arms, and that capacity is not just directed at external forces, but also against the government. The Westrogothic law, written in the 13th century, reads: "The Swedes appoint the king and also have the right to overthrow [him]." To that end, *it is necessary that the people bear arms.*

In 10th century Iceland, society was divided into various fiefdoms called goðorð, where the political leader, or perhaps head of the clan is more accurate, was appointed solely by gaining the trust of the free peasants, and the interaction between them was completely voluntary.

A political system based on the mainland tradition, which could be described as a friendship-oriented political order. This interaction also meant that the chieftain could mobilize a military force, if need be. The symbiosis between free peasants and chieftains can be viewed as support for the chieftain, who is in turn responsible for protecting the group. The exercise of authority rests fundamentally on the consent of those who are governed, in line with the original thought behind the American constitution. In other words, power was not inherited, it was elected and deserved. A parallel could be found in the Swedish kingdom, which did not depart from the Westrogothic law until our founding father and reformer Gustav Vasa ascended the throne in 1523.

The Germanic peoples employed the same system about 1,000 years before that. Both Caesar and Tacitus described the Germanic commander as elected by his men, based on valor and courage, and thus, he is loyal and humble before his soldiers.

> When a tribe wages a defensive or offensive war, chieftains are chosen to lead this war, with unrestricted power over life and death. In times of peace there is no joint government; the local leaders administer justice and settle disputes.[10]

Men were recruited from their local district, and formed a district group, a troop that was part of a larger army,

---

[10] Bello Gallico, sixth book, Chapter 23, fourth-fifth verse.

which meant that they fought side by side with members of their household – brothers, relatives and neighbors. This of course strengthened solidarity and emphasized the need to show courage in the company of your loved ones.[11] Together with other districts and their troops, the army became a whole. This was the war system (anarchic and decentralized) that single-handedly stopped the Roman invasion and punctured the Roman invasion endeavors beyond the Rhine in 9 A.D.

Locke, on the other hand, felt that the raw, beautiful power of men is "The way of the Beast,"[12] and it had to be controlled by the parliamentarian and constitutional state in order to do *right*.

However, no right can be upheld without strength, and the result of the constitutional state has become a centralization of this strength into the state, to uphold the universal right to life, liberty and property, concepts that are now being redefined by the large tyrannical masses to mean the exact opposite. The state is still the strongest force when it comes to upholding rights, and the state knows no difference when it comes to defining these concepts; it will act the same way no matter what. The constitutional, moral right to fight that which the Founding Fathers were afraid of has until now proven insufficient.

The power balance and distribution of power, *checks and balances*, are what is important. Not that it actually

---

[11] Tacitus, *Germania*, Chapter VII.

[12] Dunn, John. (1982). *The Political Thought of John Locke: An Historical Account of the Argument of the 'Two Treatises of Government'*, Cambridge University Press, p. 39.

exists in the United States today, it only pretends to – a dangerous road that the American left has mapped out for its state. It becomes the legitimate excuse for the government to exercise its power, as opposed to the original idea of a righteous exertion of power.

If the state had to take local power elites into consideration, forced reforms would become more hands-on – there would be no way to hide who is on the receiving end of policies, the muzzle would have to be aimed visibly and directly at the antagonist. Before modern states came about, all politics was intimately linked to the in-group's potential for violence. All the way from the individual level, with the connection between serving in the Armed Forces and being a citizen, back to our old ting, where the jarls and their housecarls assembled. This is what it is all founded on – to either force your own policies, or to reach a compromise that both sides can accept. This is where the commingling democracy goes wrong –it disguises itself as an expression of the latter, but is in fact the first mentioned, because all it does is keep a discussion going until a majority decision is possible. The reason is that the parties who negotiate with the ruling entity, the sovereign, lack the ability to keep the negotiation going by other means if necessary. If the in-group is not ready to maintain its own security, to look after its own interests and ensure the survival of its own identity, it will surely go under.

A positive development in this respect is the situation in Ukraine, which has resulted in an almost Roman renaissance, with political leaders that have an actual military capability. Imagine a Roman Senator who is also Commander of a legion; his words will undoubtedly have more impact than the Senator who lacks military capability. Ukraine is an extremely state-centered country, with very few libertarian tendencies, and it remains so today, but when the national army turned out to be incapable of solving the warlike situation that arose in the country in 2014, the country's saving grace was the formation of free militias, like the Azov Battalion. Today, Azov is not just a military regiment, but also directly linked to Ukrainian politics through a civil branch with the same leadership – a leadership that has declared its intention to run in the next parliamentary elections.

Using 3D-printer technology, it is just a question of time before the people, through their political units, can once again challenge the state when it comes to how much violence can be projected. When rules, in this case laws, are made, it begs the question what happens if someone breaks these rules – rules only exist within the frames of the agreement, either forcibly or voluntarily entered. The forced rule demands that a higher potential for violence be upheld, and technological advances are evening the balance in favor of the citizen.

Anarcho-fascism is the decentralized practice of government authority into the smallest possible units that can manage to maintain their own sovereignty. Every man should, as far as possible, be his own Jarl. The smallest lasting unit in a society is his family, whose well-being and safety he is responsible for – along with the other men that belong to his political unit, and he is therefore the inner as well as outer authority of the family, and its sovereign.

It is up to the man and those who stand beside him to make sure he has a potential for violence strong enough that political opponents will want to trade with him, rather than try and conquer and enslave the sovereign unit. These were the principles the Vikings adhered to – there were no raids where trade was more lucrative. The Swedish Armed Forces built their entire existence on this principle during the Cold War. The world's third-strongest Air Force secured our sovereignty by making sure it would be more worthwhile to have a dialogue with us, than to face certain death by our attack planes.

We do not have to be strong enough to replace the government power, we only have to be strong enough to stand outside it. To decide that the in-group is the exception is the final definition of being sovereign. It will be the baptism of fire of the in-group to resist the will of the other unit, and through that, cherish its own interests. To stand against the parasites of the other unit. To realize that we, using our own strengths and abilities, can stop feeding another political entity at our expense via taxes. The political unit can, in this case, be any organization, corporation, cooperative etcetera, that is forced to bear the harmful cost imposed upon them by others who offer nothing in return except a threat of violence. Many of them already offer a passive resistance to the blackmail, by moving their assets abroad. This is necessary because the threat against their assets is not made up of individual criminal elements, but the organization of the state itself. And this is just the financial cost, not the price we pay in blood. If that payment is made in full, we can never get that currency back.

The termination of the state's monopoly on violence also implicitly entails the disintegration of the fixed borders within which the sovereign has operated. A political unit such as a tribe, corporation or other interest group is not geographically bound and chained to an area, like a state is. In a best-case scenario, it will instead be mobile and overlapping.

Before private land ownership was introduced in Sweden, in the Viking era, it was the extended family that gave permission to outside parties that wanted to settle on the land they held. This practice was reformed by the church, because it wanted to be able to receive its followers' properties in the form of gifts or wills.

All this must have caused some problems, back then as it does now. How far do your individual freedom rights and your right to your own property go? Unacceptable infringements will naturally be met with violence; the clenched fist is the most obvious sign that somebody else's choices have affected you negatively. A land dispute in pre-Christian times would have been brought before the tinget, and if the dispute could not be settled there, it was resolved by single combat. This made landholders think twice before allowing people who had a negative influence on the community to settle on their lands. Society had nothing to do with the transaction between the landholder and those who settled on his land. The social cost was borne by the neighbors and the landholder raked in the profit. But because there was a risk the whole thing would end in single combat, the risk of bearing the cost was instead shifted to the one responsible for the situation.

And now for the present day relevance of all this: If a refugee center is built in a lucrative area, and it causes crime to escalate, a social cost that in turn leads to economic loss when property values start to plummet, a defense is warranted against the profiteer who counts his winnings while others bear the real expense of the transaction. Taking in refugees should be carried out in tune with society, not against it. Like the Swedes did during the Finnish Winter War, when Swedish homes were filled with Finnish children too young to stand up and fight alongside their fathers and older brothers.

The decisions of the political unit must start off from the "we" point of view. Our objectivity and the creation of universal principles have been both a blessing and a curse – they have made us grow, but also threaten to harm us when applied to the political other. They cannot extend to the others, for the simple reason that they are not reciprocal.

People in a democracy do not vote the way we wish they would, according to their common sense; they vote according to other parameters. Blacks in the United States voted for Obama because he was black, and for the same reason, we will never see a white president in South Africa again – under the current system. Neither will the United States if the demography shifts to the same extent. In that case, South Africa would no longer be the only country to have a policy that aims for positive special treatment of the black majority population, what is today known as minority rights in the United States. These rights will not disappear when the blacks are the majority, instead, they will be strengthened further until the white man has been completely crushed.

Western values, which we have obtained through the art of reasoning as well as blood, have given us the freedom we enjoy. The immediate consequence has been our superior wealth, and we will only be able to keep that if we are prepared to act against hostile political units. If we want to preserve our voluntarism, it must be limited to mainly being applied internally. Voluntarism is thereby to some extent upheld by limiting it in a universal sense. A citizen's freedom should not extend to actions that will, in the long run, limit the freedom of me and my descendants – which will be the direct consequence if the present liberal leftist establishment has its way.

Changes in society will happen from the bottom up. Human society is too complex to rule from above. Adaptive abilities improve with practice, by solving the tasks at hand. No matter what those may be. A task presents itself organically; it is focused outward, a reaction to a problem that demands a solution. It is through initiative and the entrepreneur that the results are presented, not by the top-down approach of the academic theorist.

We are so afraid of bad examples that we stare ourselves blind at the things we do not want to happen – in itself a strong indicator that they will in fact not happen. However, if they should happen, that would be a good thing. Not necessarily for the people who suffer the consequences, but for those who saw what happened. What does not kill you, makes you stronger, as the saying goes. In a decentralized society that means that those who in their own rule strengthen, for whatever reason, become a lesson to others. This is true under the current government apparatus as well. Sweden, along with Germany among others, will be a warning example to the rest of the world one day. The big difference is that in a centralized state, the mistakes are extremely costly and very hard to recover from.

A decentralized and anarchic form of government will, according to the state huggers and scaredy-cats, lead to a wild life (in a negative sense) – a society closely resembling the post-apocalyptic movies of Kevin Costner (The Postman, Waterworld), or the more romanticized Mad Max movies. I am sure we will see parts of the world move in that direction, but what we must realize is that it would strengthen the cohesion and preservation of our own community. People who live in chaos and low-trust communities observe the distinct difference between "us" and "them". The only way to become successful is to allow competition, and the most important ingredient in any competition is that it yields different results. The result is paramount, especially to the winner, and it is what allows us to say that one culture is superior to another.

We have built the most successful societies in the world. We, the people, are the precondition for those societies, not the state. It came with a price, and our ancestors paid it. What binds a society together is the trust in one's neighbor; that is what lays the foundation for what has come to be known as a high trust society – a phenomenon that exists predominantly in the West. Where your word is your bond and directly linked to your honor. This is the fundamental thing that makes transactions of valuable goods between denizens possible – you invest in each other. Your promise is your life. The Mad Max thing is for those who cannot keep their word. A man's only real legacy is his word, and therefore, it is his most valuable possession.

From the Vikings' Havamal – Odin's Song, verse 77:

Cattle die,
and kinsmen die
And so one dies one's self;
But one thing I now,
that never dies;
The fame of a dead man's deeds.

Published by Logik Förlag

Bacu, Dumitru:
  The Anti-Humans, (2016).
Berlin, Saga, Jacobson, Mats:
  Djuren i Yggdrasil, (2013).
  The Animals in Yggdrasil, (2016).
  Yggdrasil – Der Weltbaum Und Seine Tiere, (2016).
Bjurman, Sebastian:
  Flickan som jagades av elden, (2017).
Björkqvist, Björn:
  En annan bild av Hitler, (red.), (2005).
  Vägvalet, (2014)
Burnham, Stanley:
  Svart intelligens i ett vitt samhälle, (2015).
Carlberg, Carl-Ernfrid:
  Texter, dikter och bilder, (2012).
Chamberlain, Houston Stewart:
  Demokrati och frihet, (2015).
  Politiska ideal, (2017).
Codreanu, Corneliu Z.:
  Till mina legionärer, (2007).
  The Prison Notes, (2015).
Dahlberg, Per:
  Den nordiska ledartanken, (2006).
Degrelle, Léon:
  Epos, (2006).
  Fälttåget i Ryssland, (2012).
Dixon Jr., Thomas:
  Vita ryttare, (2015).
Duke, David:
  Den judiska rasismen, (2015).
  Kämpa för nordisk frihet, (2013).
  Mitt uppvaknande, (2015).

Eckehart, Meister:
Hur Sverige blev en mångkultur, (2007).
How Sweden Became Multicultural, (2017).
Eriksson, Sven:
Mod och trohet, pliktuppfyllelse och kamratskap, (2015).
Samhällets väl före egennytta: Tysk socialpolitik 1933-1940, (2017).
Faurisson, Robert:
Mitt liv som revisionist, (2007).
Revisionismens segrar, (2008).
Flodæus, Olof:
Röd död, (2012).
Garfvé, Henrik:
Ras och IQ, (2006).
Göring, Hermann:
Tyskland återfött, (2015).
Hansson, Per:
Demokratin som dödgrävare, (2012).
Harwood, Richard:
Nürnbergprocessen, (2008).
Johnson, Greg:
Nya högern kontra gamla högern, (2015).
Kemp, Arthur:
Jihad, (2016).
Kjellén, Rudolf:
Nationalitetsidén, (2009).
Nationell samling, (2016).
Kjellman, Östen:
Tankar i skogen, (2013).
Unghögern, (2015).
Vilka började andra världskriget?, (2013).
Knudsen, Harald Franklin:
I was Quisling's Secretary, (2017).
Jag var Quislings sekreterare, (2016).
Le Bon, Gustave:
Massans psykologi, (2016).
Lindholm, Sven Olov:
Svensk frihetskamp, (2012).
Macdonald, Andrew:
Jägaren, (2012).
Turners dagböcker, (2009).

MacDonald, Kevin:
    Att förstå det judiska inflytandet, (2012).
    Västerlandet och dess fiender, (2015).
Malynski, E., de Poncins, L., Evola, J.:
    The Occult War, (2015).
Molin, Adrian:
    Stafetten går vidare, (2016).
    Svenska spörsmål och krav, (2017).
Nilsson, Jonas:
    Anarko-fascism: Naturen återfödd, (2017).
    Anarcho-fascism: Nature Reborn, (2017).
Nordengruppen:
    Ett annat Tyskland, (2011).
Olfwenstam, Jan-Eric C.:
    Dold spindel, (2017).
Oredsson, Vera:
    När flaggstängerna blommade, (2016).
Rami, Ahmed:
    Tabubelagda tankar, (2005).
Rushton, J. Philippe:
    Ras, evolution och beteende, (2014).
Sennels, Nicolai:
    Helig vrede: Bland kriminella muslimer, (2017).
Snellman, Juha:
    Slavarnas tidsålder, (2016).
Svensson, Lennart:
    Ett rike utan like: Sveriges historia, (2017).
Söderman, Magnus:
    Den trotsiga, (2013).
    Till värn för Norden, (2011).
Waerland, Are:
    Känn dig själv: En studie av den svenska folkkaraktären, (2017).
Windeskog, Jimmy:
    Under blodröda fanor, (2016).

CPSIA information can be obtained
at www.ICGtesting.com
Printed in the USA
BVHW080532070720
582997BV00006B/609

9 789188 667199